M000026949

PROPOSAL ESSENTIALS
Win more, win more easily

PROPOSAL ESSENTIALS

Win more, win more easily

Jon Williams & BJ Lownie

StrategicProposals

PROPOSAL ESSENTIALS:
WIN MORE, WIN MORE EASILY

JON WILLIAMS AND BJ LOWNIE

Book design by Ciara Gilsenan

FIRST EDITION

First published in Great Britain in 2013 by
Strategic Proposals Ltd.

© Copyright Jon Williams & BJ Lownie 2013

A catalogue record for this book is available from the British Library

ISBN 978-0-9926150-0-0

The moral rights of the authors have been asserted. All rights
reserved. No part of this publication may be reproduced, stored in a
retrieval system or transmitted in any form or by any means,
electronic, mechanical or otherwise without the written
permission of the Publisher.

StrategicProposals

Proposals form a critical element of the sales cycle. This book will equip all those involved in proposal development – salespeople, subject matter experts, senior managers – with the key skills and tools necessary to develop powerful, compelling proposals. Packed with pragmatic advice from two of the world's top proposal experts, *Proposal Essentials* will help you to win more business – and to win it more easily.

"This book adds unique insights that will improve your proposals. It is definitely worth reading. Jon and BJ are always sure to light up any conference or boardroom with their enthusiasm. Their slick repartee amuses and informs in equal measures. Their combined experience is an asset to the global proposal community. They blaze a trail for others to follow."
—*Sandy Pullinger PPM.APMP, Managing Director, nFold, South Africa*

"Jon's knowledge of the world of bids and tenders is second to none. I've learnt a lot from Jon over the years and find his enthusiasm about the world of proposals inspiring."
—*Tim Barber, Director, PCD Agency*

"BJ is a pioneer in our industry who has helped define how to manage a successful proposal process across industry. His 'passion for proposals' is more than just words. Whether he is speaking at an event, serving as a mentor, consulting with a client, or writing a winning proposal, BJ gives it his all and genuinely cares about advancing our profession."
—*Melissa DeMaio, APM.APMP, Proposal team leader, global professional services firm, New York, NY*

"Jon & BJ – the perfect mix of proposal knowledge, hands-on expertise, healthy debate (mostly …), and fun. Proposal synergy at its best."
—*Martin Smith, Managing Director, Bid Solutions*

"I have been working with Jon for over 10 years in my different 'Head of Bid' roles and always appreciate his enthusiasm, expertise and wealth of knowledge. I have worked across multiple sectors and managed lots of different teams and Jon always has relevant and up to date skills and experience that my team and I benefit from. Whether in a live bid situation, a training requirement or as a sounding board / strategist, Jon meets all my bid related needs with ease and is always a safe pair of hands."
—*Kathryn Wyon, Head of Sales Advisory, Lloyds Bank, UK*

"I always find Jon, hugely positive, energetic and passionate and above all inspirational where bidding is concerned. After listening to Jon articulate any stage within the bidding lifecycle it always encourages me to challenge my process and to make improvements. Jon's experience outrivals any other within the industry that I have come across."
—Jane Matthews, Head of Bids & Tender, Aviva Life

"Jon and BJ have been a blast of fresh air and excitement since I first met them a dozen years ago. But, for me, their 'rock star' moment – that time when their audacious wit and genius combined in explosive bursts of profundity – was June 1, 2007, at APMP's annual conference in Savannah. For there, in a cavernous hall that suggested the grandest of tent revivals, they introduced me – and the few hundred others lucky to be there – to the Church of Proposal Excellence, complete with magical audience interplay, benediction and a choir. 'Believe', they proclaimed, in conclusion. 'Seek out best practice.' 'Be honest with yourself.' Since then, they've continued to evangelize – seeking truth, of course, but doing it in ways that make their associates smile."
—R. Dennis Green, Founder and former Managing Editor, Proposal Management Journal

"A master of the process and the practice, BJ Lownie also reminds us that proposals don't exist in vacuums. Through wit and shared experience, BJ teaches us that, for better or worse, it is the human equation that defines and drives the strange artifacts we call proposals."
—Dave Johnson, GauComm LLC

"Quite simply … if we need advice / help on a complex proposal, Jon is who we pick up the phone to."
—Lorraine Baird, Head of Bid, Insurance, Scotland

"Jon is a true expert in the field of Proposal Management and adds significant value to every situation he is involved in. His clear and insightful guidance, and rational thought, gives an invaluable perspective on all areas of bid management, backed up with a wide range of real world experience from both a procurement and proposal mindset."
—*Matthew Denchfield, Head of Global Bids, Canon*

"Jon and BJ are motivational, inspirational and passionate about their subject – a pleasure to work with!"
—*Janey Raine, Document Manager, Aviva Life*

"Everything I know about proposals I nicked from BJ or others who did the same. Steal this book."
—*Jeff Elkins, President, Writing Bench*

"Jon is a well-known figure in the UK proposal industry, thanks to his tireless efforts to up-skill the masses via the excellent 'Proposal Guys' blog and his links with the APMP, not to mention the excellent service provided by Strategic Proposals. He is one of a rare breed of people, someone who not only truly 'gets' proposals, but who is also genuinely passionate about them."
—*Business Development Executive, Consulting Sector, UK*

"'The Proposal Guys' – Jon and BJ to the uninitiated – are experts at clearly explaining not only how to 'do' the entire proposal process but also at explaining 'why' proposals AND process are important to everyone at all levels. Everyone buys in and then everyone wins."
—*Colleen Jolly, PPF.APMP – Principal, 24 Hour Company & Managing Director, 24 Hour Company UK*

CONTENTS

INTRODUCTION

Proposals: the power to win business

Setting the scene
The proposal: key to a successful sales campaign
RFPs, ITTs and other terminology
Can't I just start writing?

SETTING THE SCENE

So: you're about to write a sales proposal! *Good luck, all the best, may the force be with you ...*

No: hold on. This isn't about 'luck'. Sellers make their own luck when it comes to winning business.

This book will help you to develop sales proposals that maximise your chances of capturing the deal. In it, we'll cover topics such as:

· How to 'spot the winners' – we'll help you to identify and focus on deals with a high probability of winning. After all, the less time you spend writing losing proposals, the better!

· The key questions you need to ask and the activities you should undertake *before* you start to write your proposal, if you're to maximise your chances of success.

· The importance of a clear proposal strategy (and a process for developing one!).

· How to plan and structure your proposal content (*a.k.a.* 'content design' or 'storyboarding').

· Hints and tips for making your proposal writing more readable and persuasive.

Throughout, we'll provide you with simple, easy-to-use checklists that we use on a daily basis, and which have been used to capture thousands of deals around the world. Over the past twenty-five years, we've helped clients to win in thirty countries, and our win rate is over 80%.

You'll find that much of our approach is common sense. But as Mark Twain is reputed to have observed, "It seems to me that common sense isn't all that common." As long-time proposal professionals, we know first-hand that, when it comes to proposals, applying a little common sense – structured in a logical way – makes a huge difference to your chances of success.

So whether you're a salesperson writing proposals on your own or whether you're contributing content to your company's proposals alongside a team of colleagues, read on, enjoy, and learn ways you can win more and win more easily.

"Classic wisdom is customers don't select a winner, they eliminate losers. Writing a mediocre (non-compliant, non-compelling) proposal is a gift to over-worked evaluators since they will eliminate you."
—*Jay Herther (APMP Fellow / Professional & Author, USA)*

A whole host of activities takes place when you're bidding for a deal. This document doesn't discuss the sales skills needed to sniff out potential opportunities in the first place. It's not about how to hold effective meetings or workshops with potential clients. We'll leave developing the technical solution and calculating costs and pricing to the experts. We won't discuss negotiation skills. We're not going to help you to improve your golf handicap so you can impress your contacts, or to choose the right restaurants in which to entertain them!

These can all be critical to your winning the opportunity. But we're focusing here specifically on the **proposal**: the formal written document that you have to submit to a customer while you're trying to capture a piece of business for your organisation – often in a competitive situation.

The quality of your proposal will be one of several critical factors in your customer's decision-making process. When they evaluate the documents that they receive from their potential suppliers, they'll be narrowing down their options to identify the most likely winner. A great proposal can put you at the front of the pack, leaving you in the best possible position to win the business. A poor proposal will lose you the deal, and potentially cause serious damage to your reputation.

So, the goal of this book is to help you to produce a first-class proposal, which:
·   is customer-focused
·   tells a compelling story, that differentiates you from the competition
·   catches and holds the readers' attention and is a joy to read
·   is easy to navigate, review and evaluate
·   is appropriately approved
·   looks professional …
… and, as a result, maximises your chances of winning the business.

RFPS, ITTS AND OTHER TERMINOLOGY

Purchasing people come up with numerous terms for the specifications that they send to potential suppliers. You'll probably have come across documents entitled 'Request for Information' (RFI), 'Request for Proposal' (RFP), 'Request for Quotation' (RFQ), 'Invitation to Tender' (ITT) and many more. Whatever the terminology the key skills in responding successfully are largely the same.

Within the book, we'll use the phrase 'RFP' throughout as shorthand for a requirements document that you receive from a potential customer requesting that you submit specific information that will help them to choose a vendor to deliver a project. At the same time, the advice we present in the book applies equally to 'unsolicited' proposals – those situations when the client asks you to 'send me a proposal', without having issued you with a formal document to which they want you to respond.

CAN'T I JUST START WRITING?

You're no doubt eager to pick up a pen (or get your fingers on a keyboard) and start writing. All you want us to do is to get on and tell you how you can write your proposals better. Well, the advice in this book *is* what it takes to develop proposals which are more effective, more efficiently, and hence to increase your chances of success. The whole point is that it *isn't* just about writing faster and better – it's about working out what story you want to tell, and *then* articulating it superbly.

Each section of the book contains an overview of the techniques we use at each stage of the proposal lifecycle to help our clients to submit winning proposals. Over time, you'll find that most of the tips in this document become second nature – but for now, it's probably better to labour a few points to help you to build 'conscious competence' in writing great proposals that win, consistently.

The checklists we include are intended as guides; we're not advocating that you should dutifully fill in every box on every form for every opportunity. Treat them instead as a set of prompts from which you can draw the most appropriate tips at the time. This is your book. We hope you'll scribble in the margins, jot down thoughts and ideas, and make notes on the back of the nearest envelope: whatever it takes to spark your creativity and to help you to sharpen your proposals.

GIVE ME

SIX HOURS TO
chop down a tree and
I will spend the **first four**
sharpening the axe.

ABRAHAM LINCOLN

QUALIFICATION
*Choosing the right
deals to pursue*

INTRODUCTION

No-one turns up to work in the morning because they like losing. Quite the opposite, in fact – most of us *thrive* on the thrill that comes from winning business.

Losing isn't much fun: as many disappointed salespeople will tell you, there isn't a pot of gold at the end of every bidding rainbow. It doesn't do much to enhance your reputation with the customer if you trail in behind the competition. And trying to capture an opportunity uses finite and often difficult-to-secure resources: you won't score points with your management by investing time, energy and your company's money in pursuit of deals you don't win. So there's little point in spending hours (or days, or months) writing a proposal unless there's a high probability of it winning profitable business that can be delivered successfully, satisfying the needs both of the client and of your own organisation.

The starting point for a successful proposal process is knowing that you are investing your finite, precious time and resources in pursuit of the right deals – in spotting the potential winners, and steering clear of the likely losers. In other words: making an effective *qualification* decision.

To bid or not to bid? That is the question …

"I'll tell you why you lost if you can tell me why you bid."
—*Head of client's evaluation team*

THE QUALIFICATION MANTRA

Qualification is really very simple. There are four key questions that you need to answer to make an informed decision to pursue a potential opportunity:
- Is it real?
- Do we want it?
- Can we win it?
- Can we do it?

If you can confidently answer 'yes' to each of them, then you've got a winner on your hands. If your answers are 'no', 'not sure' or 'I don't know', then you may be about to invest a great deal of effort for very little (or no) return.

Let's expand on each of these four questions in turn.

- *Is it real?*

There's little point in bidding if there isn't going to be a contract awarded at the end of the day!

So if the client is considering replacing an incumbent supplier – are they *really* so disillusioned with their current provider that it's worth the cost, risk and inconvenience of change? Or is this simply a benchmarking exercise, designed to keep their existing provider on their toes and to beat them up on cost? Are they just going through the motions to show they've tested the market once in a while?

If it's a new initiative for them – does it have the right support within the customer's organisation? Do they have budgets in place? Is there a compelling event, and are there definite dates for implementation? Is this project really going to fly?

- *Do we want it?*

Is this core business for us (or an area we want to move into strategically?).

Can we make money from it: is the deal attractive for us financially, in terms of revenues and margin?

Does this create something repeatable with other clients, or that we will be able to reference in future? Will it enhance our portfolio in this area? Does it help us to build market share?

Is this a customer with whom we want to work – and with whom we'll *enjoy* working?

If we dedicate resources to this, might we have to turn away another, more profitable or interesting opportunity in the same timescales?

- *Can we win it?*

Do we have a good relationship with the key decision makers in the customer's team / organisation? (After all – people tend to buy from people they know, like and trust.)

Do we have a strong, affordable solution and can we demonstrate a proven track record in this area? Is our offer likely to be superior to those which other vendors can offer? Are their process and requirements slanted in our favour (rather than towards other likely bidders)?

Do we have a clear strategy and plan to win the business? Are we clear on who our competitors are, and how we'll be able to justify why the client should choose us ahead of them?

Do we have the necessary resources to develop a first-class proposal that will win the deal, whilst respecting the work / life balance of those who will contribute? And do we have the necessary senior management support internally?

- *Can we do it?*

There's no point in winning the deal if we can't deliver. Are we 100% confident that we have the solutions, infrastructure, expertise, management support, financing and resources available to implement our solution for the client successfully, on-time and within budget?

"A robust bid / no bid decision is the foundation for a successful outcome."
—*Jane Matthews, Head of Bids & Tender, Aviva Life*

Note that some folks would try and add a fifth criterion to the list, if they're struggling to justify chasing the deal: they have to bid, even though they know their chances of winning are very low, because 'it's strategic'. Now, there are rare occasions when this is true – if you're trying to penetrate a new market and gain experience and exposure; if you need to rebuild a relationship that was damaged during a previous unsuccessful bid; if you can explain why losing this but 'playing the game' well will put you in a strong position for a known future piece of business. But generally if it comes down to 'it's strategic', that really only confirms that this is a deal that shouldn't be pursued.

The best approach is to treat every opportunity as being 'qualified out until it's qualified in'. In other words, the default setting should be that you won't pursue a deal unless you can clearly justify why you should do so – rather than working on the premise that you'll chase anything that moves provided no-one says 'stop'!

ACTIVE QUALIFICATION

More than simply helping to decide which deals you should chase, a good qualification process will help you to identify actions that could improve your likelihood of success. We call it *active* qualification – not just a 'bid / no-bid' decision, but focused on helping you to win the deal.

Our advice? Very early on in the sales cycle – and well before any customer RFP arrives – work through the simple checklist provided overleaf:

· Assess the opportunity as objectively as possible against each of the four criteria, and note down evidence to support your rating.
· Think about where things *could* be by the time the customer takes their decision as to which supplier to select. You still have plenty of time to improve your chances in each area, so write down any actions you'd need to undertake to improve your score as far as possible.

Is it real?

CURRENT RATING	POTENTIAL RATING
YES LARGELY PARTIALLY NO	YES LARGELY PARTIALLY NO
EVIDENCE	*ACTIONS TO IMPROVE WIN PROBABILITY*

Do we want it?

CURRENT RATING	POTENTIAL RATING
YES LARGELY PARTIALLY NO	YES LARGELY PARTIALLY NO
EVIDENCE	*ACTIONS TO IMPROVE WIN PROBABILITY*

Can we win it?

CURRENT RATING	POTENTIAL RATING
YES LARGELY PARTIALLY NO	YES LARGELY PARTIALLY NO
EVIDENCE	*ACTIONS TO IMPROVE WIN PROBABILITY*

Can we do it?

CURRENT RATING				POTENTIAL RATING			
YES	LARGELY	PARTIALLY	NO	YES	LARGELY	PARTIALLY	NO
○	○	○	○	○	○	○	○
EVIDENCE				ACTIONS TO IMPROVE WIN PROBABILITY			

Whilst you're scoring the opportunity, look out for any showstoppers – areas in which you're weak now, and where you simply can't see a way to improve your scores. Double check whether these could in themselves be barriers to you winning the deal – and, if they are, then (no matter how high the other scores are) it might be worth considering a 'no bid'.

And think about the competition, too. If your qualification score is – and is always destined to be – low, then wonder whether any of your competitors would be scoring more highly. That too might give you a clue as to whether or not to proceed.

Final tip: re-qualify the deal repeatedly throughout the bid, whenever any new information comes to hand. You might glean some new insights into the customer's views of your chances of success. You may discover that one of your competitors has an inside track, or is already seen as the most likely winner. At the very least, when the RFP shows up, sense-check that your initial views were correct: it may be that your assumptions as to what the customer was looking for were actually incorrect, and that it no longer makes sense to bid. It's better to pull back from a losing bid part way through than to carry on regardless to the bitter end!

"The best way to improve your win rate overnight is to qualify qualify qualify and keep qualifying until the document is submitted."
—*Kathryn Wyon, Head of Sales Advisory, Lloyds Bank, UK*

IS IT REAL? DO WE WANT IT? CAN WE WIN IT? CAN WE DO IT?

Your qualification analysis may well determine that you shouldn't progress a particular opportunity. But how do you break the news to the customer? If you tell them at the last minute, and communicate poorly ('we don't think your project's going to work, the deal's too small, we're just not interested in the work – and we think your RFP's shambolic'), then you risk causing offence.

You'll need to make sure that you say 'no' to the client in such a way that they understand and respect your decision, and view you as being professional. Done right, this will enhance your overall reputation – thus improving your chances for future opportunities.

And 'no bidding' can sometimes actually *increase* your eventual chances of capturing the business – if the evaluators decide they don't like any of the suppliers who do actually bid, or if you can find a way to work with more senior management to try to change or circumvent the customer's current sourcing approach.

The 'no bid' discussion needs careful planning (and rehearsal). Here are a few questions to consider:

· How will the customer react when we tell them we've decided to 'no bid'?
· What does that tell us about our chances and strategy?
· Could we persuade them to change their requirements or process?
· Could we enhance our chances of success via a non-compliant bid?
· Could we circumvent their process in some way without damaging the overall relationship? .
· If we do 'no bid', what should we say to leave the customer thinking that we're professional – so that they'd want to work with us in future?
· How should we go about breaking the 'no bid' news to the customer? (Who's best to have that discussion from our side – and with which stakeholder(s) in their organisation?)

There's no point in spending time writing a proposal if you've not got a strong chance of winning good business for your organisation. A robust qualification process helps to bring a degree of objectivity to support a good salesperson's subjective 'gut feel'. It's about taking informed decisions as to which deals to chase – and hence about maximising your win rate.

So make sure you invest the time to determine whether this opportunity is truly worth chasing:

· Is it real?
· Do we want it?
· Can we win it?
· Can we do it?

(Have we repeated these often enough? Yes? Good. They're *really* important!)

Qualify early – before the RFP arrives – and again whenever new information comes to light. And don't be afraid to 'no bid': doing so professionally can actually enhance your reputation in the customer's eyes.

"Qualification? THE most important part of the Bid / Proposal process … "
—*Lorraine Baird, Head of Bid, Insurance, Scotland*

PRE-PROPOSAL PLANNING

Maximising your chances of success –
before the RFP arrives

Introduction
Pre-proposal planning: goals
Pre-RFP customer questions
Summary: pre-proposal planning

INTRODUCTION

You've qualified the opportunity, and now you're about to start writing the proposal?

Oh dear. We're too late. You see, we wanted to start you thinking about the proposal *ages* ago – long before the release of the customer's RFP.

Think about what it feels like when you're working on a proposal. You've never got enough time. You're never *quite* sure exactly what the customer really wants. You spend ages scurrying around trying to find information to include in your answers. You can never get hold of the colleagues you need to help you (or they're always too busy to provide much assistance).

So, before we start you thinking about how to turn out that elegant, flowing prose that will make your proposals a joy to read, let's give some thought to the things you can do early on – as soon as you hear that you may need to write a proposal, well before the RFP lands.

This is your opportunity to glean and gather information that might be useful when you come to write the proposal – about the customer's real needs, and their views of your organisation versus the competition.

This is the time to start to shape the evaluators' views of your strategy and solution, so that the proposal is consistent with the story that you've been telling them over the previous weeks and months. You want the buyers to open your proposal already thinking that it will be the best; you want everyone involved in the evaluation process to be favourably disposed to you. In short, you want your proposal to be sown onto fertile ground.

And there are a host of activities that you could usefully undertake internally before an RFP shows up. This is the time for you to build and brief your proposal team; to plan key project activities; to get ahead of the game by developing any content that you know you're likely to be asked for; to highlight and escalate any potential issues as early as possible.

You may hear about the deal months before the RFP is due to be released – or you may only get a few days' notice. But simply burying your head in the sand and hoping all will be well when the RFP shows up is missing a huge opportunity to wire the process in your favour – and to reduce your stress levels too!

And, by the way: if you only have a few hours' notice of a formal RFP, or first find out about it when it shows up in an email inbox – then beware! If the customer hasn't been talking to you about what's coming up, chances are, they've been talking to your competitors: you might want to think long and hard about whether it's worth bidding at all.

So ... as soon as the opportunity is a realistic twinkle in your eye – start using the materials in this chapter to maximise your chances of success.

'Pre-proposal planning' is about capturing information – regarding the customer, your capabilities to meet their needs, and about the competitive landscape – that you will need to know and use when it comes to developing the proposal.

It's about influencing the evaluators and ensuring that they'll be receptive to the proposal when they read it. (If you submit a written proposal that's full of information that is entirely new to the client, and you don't have an existing relationship with them, we suggest you don't place too much money on your chances of winning!)

And it's about doing any preparatory work that you can up-front, to ensure that you (and any colleagues who may help) have as much time as possible once the RFP has arrived to write a great proposal.

So, let's throw down the list of challenges. Before the RFP arrives, you need to be able to tick each of the boxes in the table over the page if you want to have the highest possible chance of developing a winning proposal.

DESIRED STATE BY THE TIME THE RFP ARRIVES	TICK (YES / NO)		ACTIONS NEEDED TO IMPROVE WIN PROBABILITY
1. We understand and have influenced the customer's business drivers, requirements & evaluation process.	○	○	
2. We've identified the key stakeholders in the client's organisation, and have established a good relationship with each of them.	○	○	
3. We understand the competitive landscape – and know (and have helped to shape) what the client really thinks of each bidder.	○	○	
4. We've worked out our likely solution and strategy – and the customer clearly understands what differentiates us from our competitors.	○	○	
5. We know the timescales for the RFP / proposal – and we're comfortable that we'll be given sufficient time to respond.	○	○	
6. We have a clear & realistic plan that we're going to follow to pull the proposal together, and any budget that is required has been signed-off.	○	○	

PROPOSAL ESSENTIALS

DESIRED STATE BY THE TIME THE RFP ARRIVES	TICK (YES / NO)		ACTIONS NEEDED TO IMPROVE WIN PROBABILITY
7. We've lined up and briefed the people who we expect to involve in our proposal effort, and they have set aside the necessary time to work on it.	○	○	
8. We've already started to work on any content that we think is likely to be needed in our proposal.	○	○	
9. We've identified any risks to submitting a first-class proposal on time, and taken action to mitigate those risks.	○	○	
10. The client expects us to win, and hopes that we will do so.	○	○	

As soon as you know that you're going to have to write a proposal for an opportunity, work through the checklist and see how you fare. If you're doing this far enough in advance, you very possibly won't be able to tick off many of the points – so work out what actions you could carry out to make the dream scenario come true in each area.

The earlier you start, the greater your scope to influence your chances of winning – and the more time you have available to plan for success. And the closer you are to the date at which an RFP is due to land on your desk, the more of the criteria should – we hope – be true.

How do you get the 'ticks in the boxes' on the pre-proposal planning checklist? Well, that's the art of effective account management or new business development: it's what good salespeople, senior executives and others who work in client-facing roles do for a living! You'll need to address each of the issues in turn – talking to the right people in the client's organisation (and internally) as appropriate.

The following checklist might be helpful. We're not suggesting for a moment that you pull this out in a meeting and work through it line-by-line – that wouldn't be the most subtle or skilled sales approach ever! Rather, it's a set of prompts that the sales team can use to make sure they capture the salient points before the RFP arrives.

However, if you do feel the need, we have known account managers use similar lists with a cheeky smile and 'a couple of colleagues will be helping me to write the proposal, so I want to make sure I'm crystal clear on what I tell them when I brief them: you don't mind if I run through the list with you, do you?'

"If an RFP comes crashing into email or from an on-line source weeks after release, I suggest your odds are better using your bid & proposal budget and time to buy lottery tickets."
—*Jay Herther (APMP Fellow / Professional & Author, USA)*

QUESTIONS	NOTES
1. When's your RFP likely to come out and how long are you going to give us to respond?	
2. What's the real problem you're trying to solve here (or the real opportunity you're trying to exploit?) – and what benefits do you expect to deliver?	
3. If I asked you to describe the ideal solution, what would it look like?	
4. What do you see as the main risks / challenges for your selected supplier?	
5. Do you have a budget in place for implementing the solution (and if so, what is it!)?	
6. Who'll be bidding against us – and what do you see as our key strengths compared to our competition?	
7. Are there any concerns about our ability to deliver this successfully that we'll need to address?	
8. If you had to put money on it, who do you think will win – and why?	

PRE-PROPOSAL PLANNING

QUESTIONS	NOTES
9. Who's evaluating the proposal and approving the decision as to which supplier you'll select?	
10. What will be your top five evaluation criteria?	
11. Are there any external consultants involved in the process – and, if so, what's their role?	
12. If you could picture the 'perfect proposal', what would it look like? (Content, length, layout, structure?)	

Clearly, your ability to ask these questions will vary depending on your relationship with the client. You may feel that some of the questions are uncomfortably blunt for particular situations. You may already have captured the information by other means (in which case, it can of course be useful to play it back to the client to test understanding). And you'll have your own way of phrasing things. But if they're not open to discussing the issues with you, then you might wonder whether your relationship with them is strong enough for you to win the deal anyway!

And remember: the customer is liable to be more open, less discreet and more open to influence *before* their RFP is issued than after they're engaged in a formal document exchange-and-evaluation process. Indeed, once the RFP has been issued, it's not uncommon for buyers to refuse to give any additional information to their potential suppliers beyond that stated in the documents that they've sent you, or via a very formal 'clarification' process.

There's a great deal that you can do before the customer's RFP arrives to maximise your chances of success. This section has laid out a set of challenges – things that ought to be true, if at all possible, by the time the RFP arrives.

When you do invest the time in pre-proposal planning, you'll find that when you come to develop your proposal, you'll have better information, less stress, fewer late nights, and more time to polish a truly excellent document. You will have warmed up your audience: your customer will be looking forward to receiving your document, and expecting you to succeed. And you will substantially increase your chances of winning.

"In order to hit the ground running and maximise the use of time before the RFP is due, it is essential to perform some pre-RFP planning. Ensuring the subject matter experts are available, and have as much knowledge as possible, will enable them to focus on tailoring responses to the customer's RFP, rather than spending valuable time getting to know the basics – thereby delivering a more bespoke and coherent response to the customer."
—*Matthew Denchfield, Head of Global Bids, Canon*

PROPOSAL PROJECT MANAGEMENT

*Planning and leading the
team's activities*

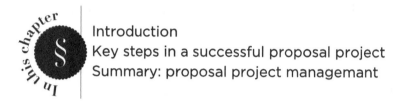

INTRODUCTION

On the face of it, developing a proposal is a tough challenge. You have a fixed deadline to hit. You need to persuade the right (often reluctant) people to help you – and ensure that their contributions are creative and high-quality. At the same time, what they see as their 'day jobs' will very probably be their top priority.

A significant number of staff may be involved, from a range of functions across the business; some of them may not have met or worked with one another prior to this project, or even have been involved in a proposal before. There's usually less time available than you'd like.

The work you're doing is sometimes highly visible to senior stakeholders internally. Several competitors will be developing their responses at the same time – and your output needs to be better than each of theirs; only a first-class proposal that is superior to the other bidders' submissions will delight the customer and win the business.

With so many challenges, and so many risks if the work goes wrong, it's absolutely essential that you treat the proposal as a 'project'. We're not going to explain basic project management theory and techniques here (but we'd hope and recommend that you would try and attend some training on this front if you're going to manage complex proposal projects). Nor is it the role of this book to teach you how to lead and motivate teams: again, we'd point you towards specialised training if you're not confident at this.

Instead, what we will do is present five major steps that you can follow to establish your proposal effort as a project, and to lead it efficiently – and to avoid the 'late nights, cold pizza' culture that characterises too many bid efforts.

KEY STEPS IN A SUCCESSFUL PROPOSAL PROJECT

We recognise that you might be writing the proposal alone. But, more commonly, you'll need to engage others to help you to develop the document. To do so, here's the plan:
1. Identify your project manager.
2. Develop the proposal management plan.
3. Identify and enlist the necessary resources.
4. Build your team.
5. Manage the project.

Let's talk about each of these in turn – bearing in mind that the same thinking applies whether you have a team working with you on the proposal, or whether you're developing it alone as an 'army of one'.

1. Identify your project manager

In some organisations, you may be able to draw on the support of a professional proposal manager to manage your activities. In others, the salesperson who owns the opportunity is responsible for leading the project.

Whatever your situation, make sure a single person, with the necessary skills and experience, is clearly identified and has responsibility for developing the plan, securing the necessary resources, monitoring progress, following the necessary internal governance and approvals procedures – and, of course developing a high-quality response and submitting it on time.

2. Develop the proposal management plan

Ideally, you'll start the project planning process before the RFP is released. You'll be identifying resources, determining capabilities and developing rough plans – as well as starting to build and motivate the team. Once the RFP is received, you can then further develop the plans, identify specific dates and determine any additional resources that you may require.

Key to the proposal plan will be the timeline, which specifies how much time will be allotted to each of the tasks associated with developing the proposal within the overall time available.

Roughly, this will fall into five phases, with strong project management essential throughout:

PHASE	TASKS	REFERENCES IN THIS BOOK
Pre-proposal	Preliminary qualification decision	Chapter 2
	Pre-proposal planning	Chapter 3
	Initial project planning and team building	Chapter 4
Initiation	Receipt of RFP	–
	Final qualification decision	Chapter 2
	Strategy development	Chapter 5
	Kick-off workshop	Chapter 4
	Document management – create a template	Chapter 8
	Content design / storyboarding	Chapter 6
Content development	Develop / write content	Chapter 7
	Document management – graphics & formatting	Chapter 8
Completion	Reviews & approvals	Chapter 9
	Document management – produce document	Chapter 8
	Document management – submit proposal	Chapter 8
Post-proposal	Proposal presentation	Chapter 10
	Learning review	Chapter 11

PROPOSAL PROJECT MANAGEMENT

As we've discussed in the previous chapter, the more work you can get done in the pre-proposal phase, the greater your chances of success. For the period between receiving the RFP and submitting your document, we'd recommend allocating the time roughly as follows:

Initiation	20% – 40%
Content development	40% – 60%
Completion	20%

Plans are worthless, but **PLANNING** *is everything.*

DWIGHT EISENHOWER

"It is first and most important to create an atmosphere where people are comfortable working together and talking together. This takes time, trust, and a strong leader. It also requires everyone to share the same basic beliefs and goals."
—*Colleen Jolly, PPF.APMP – Principal, 24 Hour Company & Managing Director, 24 Hour Company UK*

3. Identify and enlist the necessary resources

Early on, you'll need to identify the support that you'll need to pull the proposal together – and then engage the necessary team members. This may require the assistance of an executive sponsor – someone in a senior enough position to help you to secure commitment from the various functions that need to contribute to the proposal.

You'll need to speak to the contributors individually, to brief them about the opportunity and explain what you need them to do and when. You'll need to check for any potential conflicts or obstacles (such as other work commitments that might clash with your project's timescales or any personal plans such as vacations).

And you'll need to motivate them, ensuring that they are enthused and excited by working on the deal with you: this is an exciting chance for them to help to win business, not a boring drain on their time and energy.

4. Build your team

Early on in the process, you'll need to bring the key members of the team together for a 'kick-off workshop'. Ideally, the team will be able to come together in person – and that's the ideal. However, in practice, this often has to be a virtual session.

The intent of the kick-off session is to inform, motivate and connect the team. Your objective is to engender a spirit of commitment, creativity and a willingness to strive to achieve a first-class result.

This starts with team members introducing themselves to one another, and explaining their role on the proposal. The session also needs to communicate the essential information needed by project team members, including:
· an introduction to the customer, to this specific opportunity and to the competitive landscape
· a discussion of the RFP, the key requirements and the process

that the customer expects you to follow

· initial views on the proposed strategy and solution
· the specific roles and responsibilities of team members
· likely timescales and key deadlines and deliverables: what's expected by when, in what format
· the overall project plan. (This needs to be reviewed to get suggestions and buy-in from the team members, and to highlight any potential issues.)
· any major risks to the successful completion of the proposal project, and the activities needed to mitigate these risks
· conflict resolution and escalation paths: what to do should anyone need help, or be concerned about their ability to meet their agreed commitments
· the logistics: communications plans (*e.g.* regular update meetings); contact details and so forth.

5. *Manage the project*

Once the project is fully underway, it's the responsibility of the proposal manager to monitor and manage the team's on-going efforts – ensuring that tasks are completed on time.

They're responsible for heading off any potential problems that you see emerging; for resolving any conflicts as they arise; for escalating any issues; for ensuring that team members have the resources they require, and for making certain that any reviews are conducted according to the plan.

Risks to the project's success need to be reviewed regularly, and contingency plans initiated and adapted as required. The plan needs to be adjusted as necessary to keep the proposal on schedule, and any changes need to be shared clearly with the rest of the team.

Communication is key to a successful proposal team. They'll want to make sure that all those involved with the effort are kept up-to-date with key developments, and reminded regularly of major milestones; to speak to all participants frequently; to bring them together (face-to-face or via conference calls) for regular team progress meetings.

Motivation, too, is a core responsibility. With a team that may well be working long hours, juggling their proposal commitments with their core roles within the business and their personal lives, it's easy for people to start to flag. It's down to the project manager to make sure they keep spirits high, re-energise team members and continually re-focus the group on the importance of what they're doing. (This sometimes means getting the team to take a break for a few hours, even if it feels like there isn't time to do so.)

I LOVE DEADLINES.
I like the whooshing sound **they make as**
THEY FLY BY.

DOUGLAS ADAMS

"Team morale, recognition, and rewards are critical to success."
—*Jay Herther (APMP Fellow / Professional & Author, USA)*

Some proposals are written by a salesperson working solo. Many involve contributions from numerous staff around a business. Yet however large your team, every proposal is a *project*, with a fixed and often tight deadline, and it must be managed – and led – accordingly.

You need to have a plan to follow; you need to secure the necessary support and resources to hit your deadlines. And communication is all-important: team members need to be clear as to their roles, responsibilities and timescales, as well as being motivated to deliver first-class contributions.

"The very best proposals give the client an offer they can't refuse, that nirvana where their available budget and the highest quality solution actually meet. But like all the best things, nirvana isn't easy to achieve – it requires planning, planning, and more planning. Planning before the proposal is released, planning while the proposal is being created, and planning for what comes next."
—*Business Development Executive, Consulting Sector, UK*

PROPOSAL STRATEGY

*Telling a compelling story to
beat the competition*

INTRODUCTION

It's not sufficient to submit a *good* proposal to the customer: yours has to be the *best* they receive from any of the bidders. There are rarely any rewards for second place when pursuing business!

To be successful, a proposal needs to present a clear, easily-understood strategy. Put simply, to convince the evaluators to select you, your proposal needs to convince them:

Why you, why not the competition?

So, what's your story – the memorable phrase that encapsulates why they should choose you? What's the big idea?

A great proposal should have three (or at most four) memorable themes that differentiate you from the competition – so that when they close your book, the buyers are crystal-clear as to why they should choose *your* organisation.

To give you an example from a deal we helped to win for one client: they'd worked out that the key messages that set them aside from the competition were their state-of-the-art technology, and the fact they could implement the solution quicker than their competitors. The proposal strapline became: 'Tomorrow's factory, today.'

Now, we *know* that the temptation once the RFP lands on your desk is simply to start typing. Please resist temptation. The most successful proposal teams make sure they're crystal-clear on their proposal story – or *strategy* – before they start to write. We can't emphasise enough how valuable it is to step back and think about the story you're trying to tell <u>before</u> starting work on your answers! So don't be afraid of postponing, just for now.

Three thoughts, before we explore the strategy development process:

1. Many years ago, BJ coined the phrase: 'A great proposal superbly articulates a compelling story.' We'd rather you *poorly* articulated a compelling story, than that you superbly articulated something of no interest or relevance to this group of decision-makers for this opportunity!

2. When Benedict, Jon's son, was younger, he asked, 'What do you do at work, daddy?' His father's reply – not being able to offer up an easily-understandable answer such as police officer, teacher, doctor? 'I go to work to help business people to tell stories.' And as a definition of what you're doing when you're developing proposals, that's about as good as it gets!

3. Some folks dismiss the importance of developing a strategy by saying that: 'It's all about price!' Of course, if you don't present value in your proposal, *all* the customer has to go on is price – and if you're not confident your solution will be the cheapest, you'll therefore lose if you don't create value. (When you ask salespeople why they lost, they'll usually blame 'price'. When you ask why they *won*, they'll wax lyrical about their understanding of the customer's needs, the relationship they built, the compelling story they presented!) As BJ noted in a conference speech a few years back: 'If it's all about price, explain Starbucks!'

So, what's the story you want to tell?

First IS FIRST.
Second is *nothing*.

BILL SHANKLY,
LIVERPOOL SOCCER MANAGER

THE THREE Cs OF PROPOSAL STRATEGY

A clear and compelling proposal strategy is built on what we refer to as the 'three Cs' of proposal strategy:

- the **Customer** and their key drivers
- your **Capability** to deliver a solution that will meet their requirements
- the **Competition** – who'll also be hungry to win the deal.

Let's work through each of these three fundamental areas in turn, providing some structure to help you analyse what's needed to win the deal. And then we'll bring it together into an overall strategy.

When thinking about your story, you first need to immerse yourself in the world of the evaluation team to whom you're bidding:

- *Organisation*

What's going on in the customer's organisation right now? What are the key issues for their business as a whole, and for the specific area(s) of their operation involved in this particular initiative? (The more you can link your strategy to the 'hot topics' facing them right now, the greater your chances of success.)

You may know some of this from your existing relationship and previous discussions with the customer, but it's always helpful to scan any easily-accessible public-domain information too – such as their website and annual reports. And if you know that there are particular buzzwords or phrases that the customer's team use, it's worth noting these so that you can incorporate them into the proposal in due course!

- *This opportunity*

What's driving this particular opportunity? Who's behind it, what are they hoping to achieve, and what business benefits do they hope to realise? How will these be recognised and quantified?

Is there a compelling event that means that they have to deliver certain things in certain timescales? What's caused them to start doing this now (and what has stopped them doing this before?)? What would be the impact of not doing it?

- *Evaluation approach*

Most evaluation teams bring together staff from different functions within the client's organisation. So, what do we know about their sourcing process? Who are the key influencers and decision makers? What are their likely selection (or 'order winning') criteria? What are their personal aims likely to be with regard to this project? And where does the balance of power lie (for example, between the technical staff on their team and their colleagues in procurement staff).

With answers to the above in mind, you can then answer the following three (critical) questions:

1. *What do they really want?*

What is the customer looking for – in terms of 'emotion' rather than 'logic'? It's essential to get behind the specification and understand the real drivers for the project – for the client's organisation as a whole, and for the individuals on their team. As was once observed, their RFP might ask for a 'better mousetrap' – the winning proposal will be the one that truly convinces them that they'll end up with 'fewer mice'.

So try and picture yourself in the customer's shoes:
- What are their 'hopes'?
- What do the individuals in the team want to be seen to achieve?
- If you imagine yourself in a meeting at the end of the project, and it had gone brilliantly, what would they be saying about it?

We sometimes call this 'The Spice Girls question' – in honour of the erstwhile British band. Their debut song (we know you're humming it already!) was called 'Wannabe', and had the catchy refrain: 'I'll tell you what I want, what I really, really want.' That's what needs to be understood when thinking about your proposal strategy: 'Tell me what they want, what they really, really want'! Some examples of the real issues from bids we've worked on lately include:
- 'Our end-users aren't happy with the service they're getting, and we're getting lots of hassle from them. We want an easier life!'
- 'We've failed on the last two big projects we've undertaken. We really need to show the CEO that we can deliver things successfully – so this project must be on time and on budget.'
- 'We hate working with our current supplier: the relationship's poor and confrontational. We want to work with people we like and trust.'

2. *What don't they want?*

As a very senior buyer observed in one of our recent surveys:

Buyers are seeking a reasonable deal with low risk to themselves (oh yes, and their employer!)

So, again, try to get into the customer's shoes – to ensure that you show that you understand (and can mitigate) the risks associated both with supplier selection, and with delivery of the eventual project:

· What are their 'fears'?
· What keeps them awake in the middle of the night, if they're worrying about the project? Or what gives them nightmares?
· What could go wrong?
· What would be the impact on them (as a business, and as individuals) if the project failed to deliver?

3. *What will their bosses ask?*

The customer's team will need to convince their senior management that their recommendation to go with you is the correct one. As one client commented to us a few years back:

We chose you because you made it easy for us to sell you internally.

Picture the evaluation team presenting their evaluation report to their senior executives. What key questions are the folks 'on high' likely to ask about your organisation and your proposed offer, before they'd be happy to approve going with you and not with your competitors? If your story can deal with their likely issues and challenges, and will sound compelling to those with the ultimate sign-off for the project, you're in good shape.

This book doesn't, of course, seek to describe your organisation's capabilities and offerings. You should have a good understanding of these to start with – and you need to surround yourself with experts with the skills and knowledge to design the right offer for this client.

Rather, from a proposal strategy development perspective, let's consider the key thought processes you need to go through regarding your capability. There are three main things to cover:

1. List out the customer's key requirements, in order of importance. (We'd suggest sticking to their top ten or so – and asking different members of your team to draw up their own lists, then comparing notes. That way you'll get some interesting and useful debate going as to the customer's real priorities.)

2. Identify any areas of these requirements that you can do particularly well (and, especially, any that you know you can do better than your competition) – and think through how you can best illustrate this in the proposal.

3. Identify any areas of their requirements that will give you problems, and work out what you'd need to do to address these. (By the way: are any of these issues potential show-stoppers? Because if so, you might want to stop the show now and 'no bid', before you go any further. There's little point writing a proposal if you know you won't ever be able to meet some of the customer's key requirements.)

You'll hopefully have gleaned some of this from your discussions with the customer to date. You should have a clear understanding of your company's competencies (and hopefully there'll be colleagues around to help with this). Populating the following table, working through the customer's top ten requirements in turn, will help to structure your thinking:

THEIR KEY REQUIREMENTS	YOUR ADVANTAGES	POTENTIAL PROBLEMS
1.		
2.		
3.		
4.		
5.		
6.		
7.		
8.		
9.		
10.		

"Clearly understand the problem to be solved. Then and only then can you provide the appropriate solution."
—*Procurement program director, telecoms*

Next, it's really useful to map out the journey that you're going to take the customer on between now and implementing your solution. Filling out the 'transformation map' shown below will allow you to picture what it is you're going to deliver:

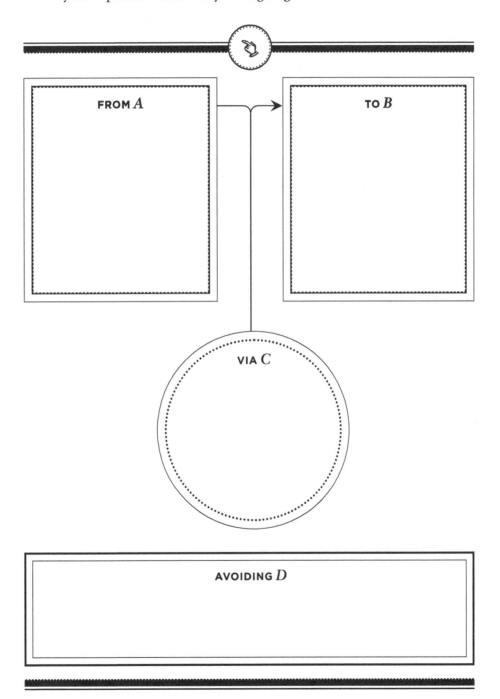

To complete the diagram, try and visualise the project as taking the customer on a journey 'from A to B, via C, avoiding D' – *i.e*:

A

Where are they today? What do they have in place at the moment? What does it feel like for them at this stage? What works – and what doesn't? What are people complaining about? If you like: what does 'once upon a time' feel like for them right now?

B

Where would they like to end up? In other words, describe 'happily ever after' from the client's perspective. (At the end of the project, what will they have in place? If you walk round one of their offices and listen to what people are saying as a result of the project, what will you hear? How will they know they've achieved success? What benefits – tangible and intangible, emotional and logical – will they have realised?)

C

What are the key activities that need to take place to achieve the change? (Don't go into too much detail – just four to six key steps that will transform their situation from where they are today, to where you're going to help them to go.)

D

What are the major hurdles that will need to be overcome (or considered) en route through the project – especially if these help you to demonstrate your experience, build trust or differentiate you from the competition? What risks will you help them to mitigate? How can your expertise and past experience help to ensure that this will be plain sailing for them?

You're writing this proposal to help to win the business.

To do that, you need to make sure that your proposal is better than that of any of your competitors.

And no matter how great your writing skills, it can be tough to be confident in your ability to be better than the competition if you don't know who you're up against, why you're better than them and hence how you might beat them.

So, to analyse your competitive position, fill in the following table:

OPTION	STRENGTHS	WEAKNESSES
YOU		
COMPETITOR ONE		
COMPETITOR TWO		
COMPETITOR THREE		

To complete this vital tool (sometimes referred to as a 'Bidders' comparison matrix'):

- List your competitors – or, at the very least, your best guess as to who else is likely to be bidding.
- Write down the top few strengths and weaknesses, as the

customer is likely to perceive them, for your own organisation and for each competitor. (What do they like about you? Do they have any concerns or reservations? What might concern them about each of the other bidders – and what might they find appealing about them?)

It also helps to rank the competitive options in order: if you had to put money on each option, who would be the favourite to win, who'd come second, and so on. This can help focus your mind on which messages you really do need to get across to beat the competitors who pose the greatest threat. (And if you think you're not the most likely to win, you might again want to ask yourself why you're investing time and effort in this!)

To develop a successful proposal, you need to make sure that the story that you tell is able to **exploit** your strengths and others' weaknesses, and **mitigate** your weaknesses and their strengths. So, step back and write down a clear list of the most important messages that you need to get across in your proposal – and how you might do so. And try to write down one word that you'd like the client to associate with your organisation and each of your competitors once they've read your proposal, if it really has differentiated you from the other options – for example:
·   You: trustworthy
·   Competitor 1: risky
·   Competitor 2: inexperienced
·   Competitor 3: expensive.

"Really understand and articulate the real business needs of the buying organization and then demonstrate how your products / services will address these needs."
—*Group procurement director, telecoms*

Out of the above, you should now be ready to work out your story: why the customer should choose you, ahead of your doubtless well-qualified and hungry competitors.

First up, determine what the client will achieve as a result of choosing you – sometimes known as your 'value proposition'. Draft a short paragraph that sums up the following:

<client> will achieve *<benefits>* by selecting *<your organisation>*

… where, as far as possible, the benefits or outcomes that you describe could *only* be achieved if they selected your organisation. For example:

ABC Limited will achieve a 40% cost saving by selecting XYZ Corporation.

Write down your strapline – the one key sentence that captures the essence of why they should choose you ahead of the competition. (Think of this, perhaps, as the title of your book.)

And then write down the three or four key messages that you want the buyers to remember from your proposal, that truly differentiate you from the other bidders. Good themes are usually snappy and superlative – the lowest risk, the most innovative solution, the best value-for-money, or suchlike. When the evaluators discuss your offer with one another – and with their senior executives – what things would truly set you apart from the rest of the pack?

This will need creativity, energy and a degree of hard work – you may 'get it' straight away, but you may need to brainstorm, scribble a few thoughts, re-write them, re-write them again, go for a walk, re-write them, pitch them to yourself in the mirror, test them with trusted colleagues or management – and re-write them again before you get something you feel happy with.

A great proposal tells a story: 'why us, why not the competition?' And you need to be clear on that story if you're going to be able to write a persuasive proposal.

You need to think about your proposal strategy *before* you start to write your document, looking in turn at each of the three Cs:
· The customer: what do they really, really want – and what benefits will they achieve?
· Your capability: how will we make this project a roaring success?
· The competition: what differentiates us?

Review these. Then write a paragraph that really summarises the benefits they'll get from choosing you – and identify your strapline and the key three or four themes that will convince them that you're the right supplier for this deal.

To be clear: it's not good enough to write the bulk of the proposal and *then* wonder what the strategy might be: you need to develop content with a clear story in mind from the very start.

WINNING
isn't everything.
It's the only thing.

VINCE LOMBARDI,
NFL HEAD COACH—GREEN BAY PACKERS

"Proposals that lack strategy, fail to win. Many proposals bore customers with irrelevant facts because they focus on informing rather than convincing. By telling a story that your customer will remember, you make it easy for them to recommend your solution. To rise above your competitors, you need a clear strategy that shows how you are unique in a way that matters to the customer."
—*Sandy Pullinger PPM.APMP,*
Managing Director, nFold,
South Africa

CONTENT DESIGN

Planning to maximise your
evaluation scores

INTRODUCTION

So, you've decide that you do want to go for it! You've done your homework. The RFP's arrived, or you've promised to send the customer a proposal by a certain date: the clock's ticking. You've got a clear strategy that should win you the deal. And now you're ready to switch on your laptop and start typing the proposal … right?

Well, we'd suggest one other key step before you start answering each question – and that's to map out the structure of your proposal, and the answer that you want to give to each question.

It's rather like building a bookcase purchased as a flat-packed kit. You can build *something* if you unpack the boxes and start bolting the pieces together without reading the instructions – but we wouldn't recommend you then line up your most fragile ornaments on the shelf below your heaviest books. That's why they include plans for you to follow, showing how everything should fit together.

And if you've ever read about how movies are developed, you'll know that companies like Pixar use a 'storyboarding' process to map out their plots – a term that's sometimes used in the proposal world too.

So when it comes to your proposal, you *can* just start typing. But you need to write the right things, not just whatever first comes to mind. So it's really worth thinking carefully up-front about how you can structure your document to make it easy for the customers to evaluate, as well as noting down the key messages you want to convey in each section and in your response to each question. This will also help to make sure your key themes are brought to life throughout the document, making it as compelling as possible.

The evaluation team is, more often than not, going to use some form of formal scoring system to mark every answer in your proposal. And if you can take a short while to design responses that really will hit the nail on the head for the readers, you're going to maximise your scores in their evaluation – and hence your chances of winning.

Moreover, as well as improving the effectiveness of your document, it will improve your efficiency – by helping you to draft great answers first time, and thus saving rework later. So whilst it might feel like you're delaying the inevitable by deferring actually typing your content for a little longer, it will save you significant time overall.

"The purpose of a storyboard is to engage your mind before the keyboard!"
—*Jay Herther (APMP Fellow / Professional & Author, USA)*

First, map out the overall structure of your proposal. This may, of course, often be largely dictated by the customer – and a golden rule for responding to RFPs is to always follow their instructions and to mirror their numbering. (Any other approach is likely to make your document difficult and frustrating for an evaluator to read, review and score – and so would be extremely high risk.)

But as a generic structure, or for a pro-active proposal (where you're not responding to a specific RFP), we'd look to include the following sections:

- *Covering letter*

A brief, one-page letter – signed by an appropriately-senior manager – thanking the customer for the opportunity to submit a proposal, and introducing the overall strategy.

- *The 'blurb'*

Provide a simple Table of Contents – with a box at the top summarising your story. At the foot of the page, include your contact name and details, a copyright statement and any simple legal disclaimers (written in as non-confrontational a way as possible!).

- *Solution overview*

As well as an executive summary – which we'll discuss shortly – it can sometimes be helpful for complex proposals to provide an overview of your proposal solution before answering their questions. This is generally more technical than the executive summary, and covers topics such as:

- Overview of their requirements.
- The potential approaches that you considered.
- The approach that you selected and why – in other words, showing that you've designed something specifically that will meet their needs.

- How you'll meet their needs – showing the benefits of your proposed approach wherever possible, as you describe the components of your solution and how everything fits together.
- Project overview – with specific dates and milestones for this client, and details of your project team's roles and their experience in delivering similar projects successfully.

- *Answers to their questions*

Provide great answers to their questions, in order, emphasising your key messages wherever possible. (See below for some specific advice on how to do this.)

If you're not responding to an RFP, but instead submitting a pro-active proposal, you'll need to brainstorm the client's key requirements and any questions that they might have in mind – and address these in sufficient detail to give them confidence that you've understood and can deliver what's needed for success.

- *Conclusions*

Finish with a summary of your story. This should be no more than one page, and mustn't contain any new information: simply reiterate your key messages and confirm your enthusiasm for the project. (It's like the old adage regarding presentations: tell them what you're going to tell them, tell them it, then tell them what you just told them!) That way, your story will be fresh in the readers' minds when they close the book.

"The proposal should ensure that all the key issues are addressed [via] a well-structured proposal, with a clear plan of how the results will be achieved."
—*Senior procurement executive, local government*

They always say that 'first impressions count', and that's true of proposals. You want to get the readers on your side from the outset, and a strong and well-written executive summary is key to ensuring that this is the case.

We can't really sum up the goals of this important section better than by quoting a senior purchasing manager we interviewed during some research into this topic a couple of years back:

> *The purpose of an Exec Summary? To blow me away so I can say, 'Yes! Yes! Yes! They really do understand my business and what I want!' A good Exec Summary shows that not only do you understand my requirements, but why you are the one to deliver them. It should provide a clear, concise summary telling me at a glance, in easy to understand language, why your offering is the best.*

There are numerous theories on structuring executive summaries; in practice, we find, it doesn't have to be complicated! Based on our research with buyers, we opt for five main sections:
· Play back the customer's objectives, key requirements and the benefits they'll achieve from the project.
· Describe the characteristics of a successful solution and supplier – slanted, naturally, in your favour: this is a great way to set traps for (or 'ghost') the competition.
· Provide an overview of your offer (which, of course, just happens coincidentally to meet everything needed for success!).
· Introduce your proposal strategy, as described in the previous section. Make sure the reader understands 'why you, why not the competition', and introduce each of your themes.
· Conclude with a brief summary of the next steps as you see them.

How long should this section be? For us, the key consideration is that you want to capture their attention *quickly*. Especially if you include some form of diagram that shows an overview of your solution and / or story, you're unlikely to do this in much under two pages – and you risk losing the reader's attention if you run to more than three! But, as ever, there are exceptions – and do take on board any specific instructions that they might give you in the RFP, and any knowledge of the customer's preferences.

We'd suggest you draft your executive summary early on in the process, and hand it to all those involved in developing the proposal. That way, you can be sure they understand your overall story and the context for what they're writing. (And then, of course, you'll need to refine it and polish it up as you get nearer to the submission date.)

"If you ask someone to contribute to a proposal and you give them a blank piece of paper, they will put it to the bottom of their to-do list, or the top of their I-don't-want-to-do-this list. They will procrastinate and try to say the dog ate their homework. Because nobody likes to start from scratch. So the best way to get contributors to contribute timely and with a quality response is to plan, take notes and storyboard. Then they 'just' have to fill in the blanks. Simple!"
—*Kathryn Wyon,*
Head of Sales Advisory,
Lloyds Bank, UK

> "If the customer wants the responses written in quill, printed on papyrus with a bow around it, please conform. Comparing proposals that don't follow the templates requested is often a long and difficult task (usually requiring additional effort from suppliers and buyers with follow up questions to clarify) and does lower the tolerance levels of those marking."
>
> —*Group procurement director, financial services*

DESIGNING AN EFFECTIVE ANSWER

How you answer the customer's specific questions will clearly depend on the RFP in question and on your organisation's capabilities. But the following approach will help you to design the best possible answer each time:

- Start by making sure you understand why they've asked the question in the first place (what does this say about their hopes, fears or needs?)
- Think through the answer you'd like to see if <u>you</u> were the customer evaluating the response. (Consider 'what's the best possible answer they could hope to receive' – using the 'three star' answer technique shown in the table below, which is adapted from an evaluation methodology used by some purchasers.)
- Think about what you're prepared to offer (and how you're going to explain any areas of non-compliance to the customer).
- Then think through which of your themes you could weave into each answer.

RATING	DESIGNING AN EFFECTIVE ANSWER
0	**'Oh dear' / 'No way'** Doesn't answer the question. Totally wide of the mark or flawed. Totally non-compliant. Lack of evidence on which to score. Not acceptable.
*	**'It's OK, but ...'** Reasonable answer. Contains most of the information needed. Acceptable but with reservations. I'd need to do more work with the supplier to refine this before I was happy with their experience and approach in this area.
**	**'That's fine'** A good answer. ATFQ (Answers the Full Question). Satisfied with this. It's workable. It meets our needs.
***	**'Wow'** They *really* understand. This is great: they appreciate our issues and aims. There's real innovation and originality here.

If you're struggling to unlock your creativity for any question, we use a technique called 'Questions to answer questions', shown on the following page. Try it: it will help you think through what you might want to say.

QUESTIONS	NOTES
1. Why have they asked this question?	
2. What are their real underlying issues & concerns?	
3. Which member(s) of their evaluation team will be particularly interested in this question?	
4. How important is this question to them?	
5. What competitive advantages can we exploit?	
6. What competitive disadvantages do we need to mitigate?	
7. Which of our themes can we bring out here?	
8. Which other questions are closely related?	
9. What existing, pre-written proposal content can we adapt?	
10. If this was *the* one question that mattered, and we were equal with the nearest competitor on every other issue, what would we say?	

PROPOSAL ESSENTIALS

Based on your response to these prompts, you should now be able to note down a rough outline of the information that you're going to include in your answer.

> "Some [proposals] are articulate, really have got under my skin, are really convincing – whereas others look mechanical, dull, pre-written and could have been meant for anyone."
> —*Procurement director, insurance*

A MAP OF YOUR PROPOSED CONTENT

If you're working on the proposal on your own, you can scribble your thoughts on each answer in the margins of the RFP. If you're working as part of a *team* developing the proposal, you may find it useful to use a structured approach to collate notes on the proposed content from each contributor. Without this, developing your proposal will be like completing a jigsaw without the box – a clear picture might eventually emerge, but the process will be unnecessarily daunting and time-consuming.

For larger deals, we'd therefore recommend that you produce a section-by-section outline of your key messages – for example, using the simple template overleaf:

SECTION TITLE	KEY MESSAGES	SECTION OWNER	LENGTH (PAGES)

We're not suggesting that you write *detailed* content at this stage: just that you capture some bullet point notes summarising what you're going to say in each section. That way, anyone involved in the proposal can see at a glance what's being covered in the document as a whole – and you can check for consistency and to make sure your solution's really going to come to life.

And then, for each section, work through each question or requirement in turn, recording brief notes on what's going to be said in the proposal:

QUESTION	KEY MESSAGES	THEMES			OWNER	LENGTH (PAGES)	NO. OF GRAPHICS
		1.	2.	3.			

You'll see that there are columns for each of your win themes: you can then check which of your key messages are emphasised in each answer, to make sure each theme really is coming through sufficiently strongly in the document. If you have time, you can also go back to the analysis you did on the three C's – Customer, Capabilities and Competition – when you were developing your strategy, and double-check that you've captured all of your differentiators at some point in your outline answers.

And you'll see that as well as setting out the rough length of the answer, you can try to record how many graphics (diagrams, tables, illustrations *etc.*) would be included – simply as a prompt to make whoever owns each answer think about visuals as well as words.

Time permitting, you can then give this high-level storyboard to relevant experts and senior managers in your business, so that they can review it. Capturing their good ideas at this stage – and getting them bought into your proposed content – is a great way of avoiding last-minute chaos later in the proposal when they get first sight of a draft document and make 'helpful' suggestions that have to be incorporated far too late in the process!

SUMMARY: CONTENT DESIGN

If you want to win, you're going to need to score as highly as possible when the customer evaluates your proposal alongside those of your competitors.

By structuring the proposal effectively – from a powerful executive summary, right through to an effective conclusions section that leaves the reader 'on a high', you'll get your story across as effectively as possible.

And by considering how you can present your responses in a way which appeals to the customer as much as possible, you'll significantly ratchet up your scores in their evaluation. This may all sound cynical and calculating. And that's because, to an extent, it is. But it works – and as you *can* work out how to score higher in the customer's evaluation process using these techniques, why wouldn't you?!

"Of the proposals received, at least 15% do not actually answer the questions posed, and try and shoehorn a ready-made answer to almost any question. The best proposals have answered the questions without the hard sell, but have woven into the bid reasons why you want to do business with that organisation."

—*Head of IT procurement, retail*

"An early content design meeting will enable contributors to remain focussed on the solution and client benefits, and remove the temptation to fill the blank void with generic boilerplate text of no value to the customer."

—*Matthew Denchfield, Head of Global Bids, Canon*

CONTENT DEVELOPMENT

Bringing your story to life

Introduction
Top tips for proposal writing
Sharpening your content
Summary: content development

INTRODUCTION

You've done most of the hard work already: you've got a clear, compelling strategy and a story to tell. You know the key messages you need to present. You've worked out how to structure your document, and you'll have storyboarded an outline of what you need to say in each section and answer.

All you need to do now is actually pull the information together, and articulate it effectively. And *now* we're going to let you start writing!

So, how to develop persuasive, easy-to-read, easy-to-evaluate content? This section offers tips for proposal development that are simple to apply, yet which will make a huge difference to your documents.

"We also don't weigh the proposal and reward on how heavy or how thick the proposal is!!!! Much rather a smart, slick proposal than a 1000-pager."
—*Group purchasing director, FMCG*

"Preparing writing guidelines for a joint bid with a large partner proved to be invaluable as we all used the same terminology and kept the messages consistent across the different sections – and significantly reduced the editing effort."
—*Edel Barnard, Proposal Manager, SITA*

"Less is more. Avoid 'me' proposals and write to the evaluators."
—*Jay Herther (APMP Fellow / Professional & Author, USA)*

A great proposal is a joy to read.

Now, everyone has their own writing style. It's important that you write in a way that feels natural and that conveys your enthusiasm for the opportunity in question, and for your organisation.

But there *are* proven techniques that can ensure that your proposal writing is as effective as possible. It's not enough to simply provide any old answer to fill the gap on the page: each response will score you points in the evaluation (or compromise your credibility) and so needs careful crafting.

1. **ATFQ** (Answer The *Full* Question): first and foremost, provide a straightforward, clear, easy-to-understand response – ensuring that you don't miss any information out, that you answer each element of the question clearly and in the correct order, and that answers only contain relevant material. It may sound obvious – but buyers report that the single biggest way that bidders throw away marks is by trying to shoehorn any old material into an answer (even if it doesn't quite address the specific question at hand), rather than being specific and focused.

2. Write **customer-centric content** – write to and about the customer, not for and about yourself! If you count up the number of times you mention the customer by name (or 'you', 'your', 'yours'), you should find yourself talking about them at least twice as often as you mention your own organisation (by name, or 'we', 'us', 'our', 'ours'). When Jon's son Benedict was tiny, his first ever words were, 'Me, me, me.' Too many proposals are like that!

3. Follow the **left-hand rule**: if you scan down the left-hand column of the page, you should see more mentions of the customer's name than of your own. That shows that you're thinking of the customer first and foremost.

To do this, present **value and benefits first,** before explaining the features of your solution; don't hide them away in the text or use them as the conclusion to your response. In journalistic terms: 'Don't bury the lead'. You want to start with 'they lived happily ever after' rather than 'once upon a time'!

And use the **'so what'** test: check that the benefits to the customer are clearly stated – don't just write about the features of your solution. Your response should complete the statement: 'What this means to you is ...'

4. **'Prove it'.** Back up the claims you're making in the document with tangible, verifiable evidence. Provide as many quotes, case studies and references as you can to build credibility. It's all very well *you* claiming you can do things well; it's far more powerful if you can provide independent proof points and examples to support your story.

5. Highlight differentiation from competitors, by emphasising your strengths and subtly drawing attention to their weaknesses (known as 'ghosting'). But **don't use direct 'knocking copy'.** (Use *e.g.* 'We initially considered XYZ but rejected it because ...' rather than *e.g.* '123 Co.'s solution is fundamentally flawed in the following ways ...')

6. Use **active sub-headings** – such as 'Delivering the project on time' rather than simply 'Project plan'; 'A skilled, experienced team' not 'Project staff' – thus telling a summary story when the reader scans through the document and conditioning them before they dive into the answer.

7. Vary paragraph length, but adhere as far as possible to the **'rule of thumb'**: paragraphs should typically be no longer than a bent-over-thumb's length when printed out – that is, about an inch (or 2.5cm for the metric readers amongst you). Otherwise there's too much information for the reader to absorb without being tempted to start skipping over your text.

8. **Keep sentences short.** Guideline: 15–20 words, with some variation. Once sentences get anywhere near 30 words, it becomes tough for the reader to absorb the information you're trying to convey. (And the first and last sentences of each paragraph should ideally be shorter: 7–11 words.)

9. **Keep it concise.** Check what you've written, and ask what it *really* adds to your story. If it's not relevant, don't include it.

   We loved the feedback we had on a proposal we helped with a while back: 'Your proposal said twice as much as the one from your nearest competitor, but was half the length.' Remember the old adage attributed to Mark Twain: 'I didn't have time to write a short letter, so I wrote a long one instead', or the scathing comment from writer and critic Ambrose Bierce: 'The covers of this book are too far apart!'

10. Make the **length of answers appropriate** to the importance or complexity of the question. If your answer seems very long or complicated, remember to ask yourself, 'What are we <u>really</u> trying to say here?' – then say it! You'll usually find that helps you to see the wood from the trees!

11. Avoid sending evaluators on a 'scavenger hunt'. Answers should be complete in and of themselves: **don't re-direct the reader** unnecessarily to other sections of the document.

   If you have to cross-reference them to avoid disrupting the flow of the document, provide enough of a synopsis of the material they'll find in (say) the Appendix to enable them to give you a high score for the answer without wading through pages of attachments. (One proposal we critiqued for a client included the memorably awful phrase: 'Detailed biographical details are included in CVs in Appendix C and in Tables 3a, 3b, 4a, 4b, 4c, and 5 and in Appendix G.')

   Along similar lines, only include website addresses (URLs) where the very presence of the information on the Web is

CONTENT DEVELOPMENT

in itself a selling point: in this case, provide screen shots of relevant pages and summaries of the information they contain within the body of the text.

12. Ensure that the document reads easily, in a style with which the evaluators would be comfortable. Make sure your text is **personal and conversational**: imagine that you had to read your answer aloud to the evaluator: would it come across as natural, engaging, friendly? You need to be confident and authoritative – not complacent or arrogant.

So throw away the thesaurus and **use simple words and phrases** – you're trying to win a bid, not the Nobel Prize for Literature!

13. Keep the document **free of clichés and jargon**. Use acronyms sparingly, and explain terms in full the first time they appear in the document. Where readers encounter terminology that's confusing or unfamiliar, it's likely to jar with them and switch them off.

14. Do, however, include common 'buzzwords' used by the customer where appropriate – and whenever possible **mirror the language** that they use in conversation and in their RFP.

15. **Give a straight answer** to a straight question – if they're asking for a 'Yes' or 'No' answer, make sure you give an unequivocal response. But then provide evidence to back up and explain your answer. And if you are non-compliant, be honest – and if appropriate try to explain how your approach will deliver the client the same (or greater) benefits, just in a different way.

16. The proposal **should speak with one voice** throughout, with different sections consistent in terms of style and substance, rather than reading like the collected jottings of disparate enthusiasts within your organisation! (If you have a team of contributors, this will require you to brief them up front on

the style you want them to use – and on some of these hints and tips – as well as necessitating careful editing of what they've written and contributed.)

17. If you use content that has been 'lifted' from previous proposals, or extracted from a library of pre-written proposal content, do **tailor any 'boilerplate' text** to the needs of this specific customer and opportunity. Include their name; refer to meetings you've had with them, past projects you've delivered for them or details of their locations; quote specific dates. Make sure everything feels focused on what you'll actually deliver for them and when: tell them what you *will* do in practice, not what you can do in theory.

18. Use **bold statements**. Only 'fudge' your assertions ('We think ...', 'We believe ...', 'According to our understanding of your requirements ...') where strictly necessary. And if you do need to qualify your statements, do so at the end rather than the start of your sentence – *e.g.* 'Our solution will deliver the results needed, according to the information available to us.'

19. **Avoid 'inadvertent risk'** statements (*e.g.* 'we guarantee that ...'). When trying to write impressive, customer-centred prose, it's easy to accidentally create expectations that you may then struggle to meet, or make commitments that might prove hard to live up to.

20. **Use tables, call-out boxes, numbered lists and bullet points** to make the text more readable and to highlight key messages. Vary their use – but be careful not to over-use them. You don't make the document read like a PowerPoint presentation pasted into Word, suffering from 'bullet-itis'.

And remember – *every* answer is an opportunity to reinforce your story, creating empathy with the customer and differentiating you from the competition.

"Buyers are not idiots. They read good proposals thoroughly and they are not amused at fluff, being patronised, inconsistency, arrogance or shabby editing."
—*Capital & construction director, government department*

SHARPENING YOUR CONTENT

Truly powerful content is *developed*, not merely written. The first version of text that gets produced will be far from perfect, so you'll need to build time into your plan to review, edit and refine it.

Whether it's for a large, complex response or for a much smaller one, we use a structured process to develop material, the steps of which are as follows:

1. **Initial review** of the first draft answer. Get someone other than the author of the content to read it; let them critique it, and then try to refine it incorporating their feedback.

2. **Editing.** Not everyone can write brilliantly. If you want to produce a first-class proposal, you need to have someone who writes well and can polish your script. (If you can't do this yourself, consider using a professional writer / editor or find a colleague who writes especially well.)

You need to make the writing 'tighter' – removing unnecessary words, and sharpening your sentences and paragraphs. You need to work on the language aspects of the content – grammar, word usage, punctuation and spelling. You need to make sure that the text from different contributors reads with 'one voice'. And then you need to check back with the original authors, to make sure you've not inadvertently changed the *sense* of the answer in any way.

3. **Proofreading.** Everyone has a tale to tell about a spectacular, inadvertent error in a document they've read – the sort of thing that Word's spell-check doesn't pick up. (One recent favourite of ours was the proposal that talked about the organisation's project management 'mythology', rather than 'methodology'. Another noted that, 'We always lie to satisfy our customers'.)

   Now, buyers are human too, and the odd minor error in a document will probably be tolerated – but the more mistakes you make, the more it chips away at your credibility (and, hence, chances of success), and the more frustrating the document will be to review. A proposal containing numerous errors will cause the evaluators to question your professionalism and, by extension, to doubt your ability to deliver a solution successfully for them.

   As you're probably aware, it's almost impossible to proofread your own document – since you're too close to the text, and if you didn't know a particular rule of grammar when you drafted the answer, it's highly unlikely you'll have learnt it in the intervening few days. So ask a colleague to read through it for you (being sure to choose someone who has sound attention to detail, the ability to focus, sufficient time and a good command of the rules of English). The goal? There should be no errors in spelling, grammar, punctuation or layout.

   Practically, proofreading should be the last activity to take place before you close off and print the document – in other words, it should come after you've incorporated feedback from

CONTENT DEVELOPMENT

the peer review (or 'red team') discussed in section 9 below. We've included it here, though, for ease as it's part of the content development process.

In certain *kinds*
of writing ... it is normal
to come across
long passages which are almost completely
lacking in meaning.

GEORGE ORWELL

"Often volume is prominent over differentiation or smart approaches to address needs and provide solutions. Along with the volume often came the 'corporate cut and paste' stuff purely puffing up the seller with no 'bespoke' relevance to the buyer."
—*Procurement director, mobile telecoms*

Write concise content that's customer-centric, backed up with plenty of proof-points, in straightforward and easy-to-understand language.

And try to follow a structured approach to developing your content: material from your contributors will need to be reviewed, refined, edited and proofread before it's sent to the customer.

"At business school and in grammar classes, we learn to write long sentences with big words that sound important. I often see proposals that fall into the trap of trying to sound too clever while failing to say anything that matters to the customer. As the speed of business accelerates, so our proposals must become easier to digest quickly. They also need to keep our attention and stay in our minds after reading."
—*Sandy Pullinger PPM.APMP, Managing Director, nFold, South Africa*

DOCUMENT MANAGEMENT

*Producing a proposal that
is easy to review*

Introduction
Effective proposal design
Producing your document
Summary: document management

INTRODUCTION

We've been talking a lot about the *written* content of your proposal. Somehow, too, the material that you produce is going to need to get to the customer on time – as a complete, compliant, well-formatted document.

'Document management' is the art of pulling together a well-designed proposal that is easy to review and navigate, and which enhances the customer's impression of your professionalism.

Effective layout and design will greatly enhance how your proposal is received and, in turn, help to improve your score. But style won't count for much if the substance is flawed – or if you end up missing deadlines, submitting incomplete documents, or making other basic errors that undermine your professionalism in the eyes of the customer.

So in this chapter we're going to explore two areas: the look and feel of your book, and the process you need to follow to produce it.

The better laid-out your proposal, the easier and more enjoyable it'll be for the customer to evaluate – and the more it'll stand out from the crowd. Here are a few golden rules for proposal design:

1. *A high-impact front cover*

A professional-looking cover can help your proposal to create the right impression from the start, differentiating your document from those of your competitors.

Make sure the customer's name or logo is somewhat larger and more prominent than yours. Include a photograph or illustration, relevant to the client and / or your story. And include a strapline that summarises your story – not just 'Response to RFP' as that's no different than, well, putting 'novel' as the title of a work of fiction!

In some cases – especially for more strategic deals – it's worth generating a highly-tailored front cover using professional designers. For example, bidding to a media conglomerate, we developed a cover that mimicked the layout of one of the newspapers they publish: they were hugely impressed.

2. *A consistent layout*

Make sure the styles and conventions you use are consistent throughout the document, from section to section, including:
· page layout – including margins, headers and footers
· section numbering
· headings and sub-headings – font, size and colour
· body text – font, size and colour
· bullets
· colours within tables, charts and other graphics
· labelling and numbering for graphics.

In the best case, your company will have standard templates available that you can re-use and adapt for each proposal – since setting these up requires a fair degree of skill both in design and in word processing / desktop publishing terms too.

3. Use white space

A designer we once worked with used the phrase: 'Give your text room to breathe.' Too many proposals are too cluttered, too dense – and hence become hard on the eyes for the evaluators.

Don't be afraid to include plenty of white space – between answers, and between sections. It makes the document easier to read, and also provides much-needed space for reviewers to jot down notes or comments.

4. Use bold to highlight key phrases

As the reader scans through a document quickly, their eyes will come to rest on headings, graphics and any bold text. Use this to your advantage: highlight key phrases or messages in bold, to make them stand out prominently and stick in the evaluators' minds.

Don't over-use this, mind: only use bold for a few really important phrases, otherwise the reader will tire of it and the bold text will lose its impact if it's used for material that doesn't warrant the extra emphasis.

5. Break up the flow of text

Documents that consist of page-upon-page of solid text are tough going – even if the writing's engaging and interesting. If text isn't broken up with effective visuals, people start to skim rather than really reading. And that could result in your readers missing critical information and your proposal being awarded lower scores than it deserves.

So make sure that every double-page spread of your book has at least one visual – a table, chart, graph, photograph, call-out box or diagram – that breaks up your text.

6. Use graphics

They say that 'a picture's worth a thousand words'. Certainly it's true that people absorb and retain information better if they're presented with illustrations as well as text. Whenever we work on a proposal answer, we ask the question: 'Is there a picture that would bring this to life?'

Not just any old illustration, mind. There are a few key tips to follow:

· Wherever possible, make your graphics specific to this customer and opportunity.

· Make the customer (and their concerns, or the benefits they will achieve) the centre of attention in any diagram.

· Illustrate the benefits to the customer wherever possible. (For example, one recent draft proposal had an organisation chart of the bidder's help desk; drawing a picture to show that 'we fix any problems quickly and professionally' made it so much more powerful.)

· Keep your illustrations simple and uncluttered. It's 'a picture tells a thousand words', not 'a picture filled with a thousand words'. Designers talk about the 'ten-second rule' – if you can't fully absorb what a diagram's trying to say in ten seconds maximum, it's too complicated. And if you have to explain it, that's a good sign that the graphic isn't as clear as it needs to be.

· Use colour – but make sure your picture would still be legible in black and white (if the customer took a photocopy, or printed from an electronic version of your document).

· Provide a simple caption that helps the reader to understand the key message that your picture is trying to convey. (We're very wary of over-lengthy captions: they tend to disrupt the reader's flow through the document, so keep labels to a short sentence at most.)

· In longer or more complex proposals, consider numbering your graphics in order – *e.g.* 'Figure 3.4' being the fourth graphic in section three. (Some folks would insist that you do this in every proposal; we think it's probably overkill for simpler documents, and makes them feel a bit academic or theoretical.)

- Check graphics especially carefully. 'Spell check' won't spot errors in graphics, so be careful to give them particular proofreading attention before incorporating them into the proposal document.

7. *Use headers and footers carefully*

We'd generally expect every page to include the client's logo, your logo, a page number and the title of your proposal. (Think about it: if they've sub-consciously noticed your strapline on the bottom of every page of the document, even the most obstinate evaluator will be likely to remember it!)

We'd not expect to see confidentiality or copyright statements cropping up in every footer – unless there are very specific legal reasons for including them in particular markets.

8. *A professional back cover*

If your design skills are up to it, why not also include a professional-looking back cover? If you buy a book in a store, the back generally gives you a synopsis of a plot and a few positive quotes.

You can use the same technique for your proposal – with a line or two introducing your story, and (perhaps) a quote from a senior manager underlining your commitment to delivering the project successfully.

"It takes 40% less time to explain complex ideas using graphics: when producing a proposal, good graphics can give you a real advantage."
—*Tim Barber, Director, PCD Agency*

"They say a picture tells a thousand words and we always find this to be true in our responses. Think about a document or a 'text book' that you would want to read (not a novel) ... You don't want to pick up something that is monochrome with pages and pages of unbroken text – so your reviewers won't want to either! Break up your pages, make it look good, include white space and a bit of colour where you can and definitely include good, relevant graphics that easily tell your story for you."

—Kathryn Wyon,
Head of Sales Advisory,
Lloyds Bank, UK

At its simplest level, the remit of document management is to ensure that the customer receives the right number of documents, of an appropriate standard, in the desired format, in the correct timescales.

The realities of life in most businesses mean that, even if you have an in-house proposal team, they may not always be able to provide dedicated document management resources to help on each and every proposal effort. It's not uncommon for members of the account team, or administrative staff, to be pressed into service to 'tidy the document up and print it off'. Whoever is providing your document management support, you'll need to follow the key steps below if you're submitting hard copies of your proposal:

1. Identify the customer's documentation requirements

What has the customer asked for in their RFP in terms of the document logistics: how many copies, what information must be included, where do they need to be sent, by when, what electronic copies need to be sent or uploaded, *etc. etc.*?

2. Develop template

Set up an 'empty' proposal – a professional-looking layout that incorporates the customer's questions, leaving space into which your answers can be inserted.

When designing your template, think about the image that you want to portray with your document: an innovative solution may call for a more exciting layout than if your story is 'proven and trustworthy'.

3. Insert answers into the template

Ensure that the content that is developed is inserted correctly into the document as it's produced, and that it's formatted as required. Keeping careful track of this is essential, to make sure that you don't lose track of the latest version of each piece of material! A simple spreadsheet listing who's providing what and when may well help, for more complicated proposals.

As a general rule, if you have multiple contributors to the document, it helps if one team member is given responsibility for the control of the document. This person should be the only one moving content into the 'master' document, thus ensuring that only the appropriate information is going into it, and that you can always get hold of the very latest version of all of the content. (We both know we're doing our job right when leading a proposal effort if our document manager refuses to let us go into the master copy!)

And do take regular back-ups of your document: it would be a nightmare if you only had one copy, and it somehow got corrupted!

4. Check document

Print out the document and check the layout carefully before you come to print the final version. Key things to look for include:
- section numbering
- cross-referencing
- table of contents
- pagination.

When you're done, you'll have a final draft and be ready to print the master copy.

5. Print document

Produce the necessary number of printed copies for the customer and for internal use – and produce CDs or versions to email if required (in PDF format, unless stated otherwise).

If you're able to, we'd strongly recommend that you use a trusted external printer to print your document. They'll do it quicker and more cost-effectively than you; it'll reduce your stress levels; the final output will invariably be of a higher quality.

We also strongly advise that you use environmentally-friendly materials for your proposals and packaging – at least, printing them on paper from sustainable sources.

6. *Check output*

Turn the pages of the copies that have been printed out, *before* they are packaged up to be sent out to the customer, and add in any necessary additional materials (CDs, business cards, requested attachments, brochures *etc.*).

And check carefully that any electronic copies that you may be sending open easily and display correctly on the screen.

7. *Package the documents*

It's worth giving careful thought to the packaging in which you ship printed copies of your proposal. A cheap envelope from the stationery cupboard, with a hand-written address, is unlikely to make a positive first impression on the recipient!

The outside of your package is the first thing your customer is going to see, so this should be labelled clearly and neatly and in line with any customer instructions. And do make sure you've included all of the materials that you wanted to send: have a packing list to hand to check that everything's been included.

8. *Deliver document*

Ensure that the documents are sent to the customer allowing sufficient time for delivery – via hand-delivery, courier, e-mail *etc.* – and ensure that timely receipt is acknowledged. A signature on delivery should always be required from the customer – even when the proposal is hand-delivered!

"A strong design and professional production of your bid document demonstrates confidence, a desire to win, empathy with your clients' needs and enforces your key messaging."
—*Iain Moring, Managing Director, Screaming Colour*

"Graphics are not better than text and text is not better than graphics. Graphics without text leaves room for ambiguity. Text without graphics hides your solution in a sea of words. Graphics and text should work together."
—*Mike Parkinson, Principal, 24 Hour Company*

REVIEWS AND APPROVALS

Improving and approving
your content

Introduction
The power of a peer review
Confident you can deliver
Summary: reviews and approvals

INTRODUCTION

No matter how good the proposal you've developed, you'll always find that someone reading through it afresh will come up with useful suggestions. A peer review process – with a few trusted colleagues offering constructive suggestions having read a near-final version of your proposal – is therefore a great way to fine-tune your document and improve your scores.

It's also important that you have the backing of your organisation for the offer that you're about to submit. In other words, you want to be sure that you have senior-level approval for your solution, the implementation plan, the financials, and the commercial and legal aspects of your response – based on a clear understanding of any assumptions you've made and any risks you've identified.

Both of these activities need to take place late on in the process – once your offer has been finalised and the majority of your content developed; in time for any feedback to be incorporated and for final checks to take place in good time before the proposal has to be submitted to the customer. You shouldn't find that there are major, fundamental issues emerging at this stage – rather, it's all about having appropriate checks in place to make sure you're going to win good business that you can deliver successfully.

"There is always a 'Red team' review — it's better if it's done by your company rather than the evaluators!"
—*Jay Herther (APMP Fellow / Professional & Author, USA)*

THE POWER OF A PEER REVIEW

Proposal teams who are serious about winning invariably schedule time to have their documents independently reviewed shortly before they're submitted to the customer. A fresh pair (or, ideally, pairs) of eyes can quickly highlight areas in which the proposal could be improved, thus enabling you to make changes that will ratchet up your scores in the customer's evaluation.

Select reviewers who understand what a good proposal looks like. If they've worked in purchasing, that's a bonus – as is any knowledge of this specific customer. And try to ensure that they have a reasonable understanding of the products and services that you offer – albeit one of the tests during a review is whether you explain your solution clearly enough to someone who's not familiar with your offerings. Perhaps pick a few senior managers whose teams would be involved in the implementation – as well as senior sales management who are accountable for helping you to win.

Brief them carefully about the customer's requirements and the competitive landscape. But don't tell them *too* much – you want them to be open-minded when they pick up your proposal.

Provide them with the RFP; encourage them to read through it thoroughly and to use it as a basis for their review of your proposal (to check you've followed all of the necessary instructions, and that the responses are compliant with their requirements).

Ideally, the version of the document that you provide for them to review should be in near-final format: there's no point in having them review a document that's a long way from completion.

Be realistic about the time the review requires: don't rush it. Ask them to be specific in their feedback: request that they provide constructive suggestions as to how you could improve your content and hence your scores – highlighting what needs changing and how it might be changed, rather than simply stating: 'I don't like this answer'! Make sure they flag any high-priority suggestions very clearly.

If you can't get them to give feedback face-to-face, then asking them to record their comments on a form is a good idea, to make it easy for you to pass their feedback on to the relevant contributors. Meanwhile, discourage them from focusing on proofreading: whilst they might spot a few typos in passing, that's not really where these reviewers can add the greatest value.

And be sure to allow *yourself* sufficient time to incorporate their suggestions into the final version of the document.

In the proposal world, especially in the government sector, this is sometimes known as a 'Red team'. We happen to think this is unnecessary jargon, but if you hear the phrase bandied around, at least you now know what those folks are talking about. But whatever you call the review, having your proposal critiqued by people who are on your side before the customer's team gets their hands on it will greatly help you to fine-tune your messages and correct any mistakes. It's a stage of the process that we highly recommend you follow.

Several years ago, we asked a proposal manager working in the financial services industry to describe the scariest moment of a bid their team had just won. 'The scariest moment?' he replied. 'That's easy. It was the moment the customer phoned up and told us we'd won, and we realised that we were going to have to deliver all the things we'd made up for the proposal at three o'clock in the morning as we rushed to get it completed on time!'

It should go without saying that there's little point in winning business unless you can deliver it successfully and profitably. That's why your proposal needs to be approved by relevant senior management before it's submitted to the customer.

Some companies have highly structured bid approval or 'governance' processes. At the very least, we recommend asking your manager, plus the person responsible for the particular areas of the business that would deliver the solution should you win, to review the details of your offer. The key things they need to agree to and validate are as follows:

- Is the solution complete, correct, clear, compliant and robust?
- Are the delivery timescales reasonable and achievable, and do we have the resources to deliver?
- Do the financials look OK?
- Are the commercial terms acceptable?
- Have all of the risks and assumptions been identified and stated, and are they comfortable with these?
- What else, if anything, could be included that could improve our chances of winning? Put another way: are you doing *enough* to win?

If you've followed the process we've outlined here, this final review and approval by your key stakeholders should be something of a formality, as they'll have been consulted as you've developed the document. At this stage, you want them to be rubber-stamping the offer, not redesigning it at the last minute. And beware: no matter how good you become at this, there's always going to be some bright spark who wants to add 'just one more thing ...' at the very last minute. (Your task is to do everything in your power to capture their input and creativity so much sooner!)

But sending the document to the client without the confidence that the powers-that-be in your organisation are comfortable with what you're offering is risky (and, potentially, career-limiting should anything go wrong when it comes to delivering what has been offered in the proposal!).

SUMMARY: REVIEWS AND APPROVALS

Once you're close to finishing your proposal, ask a small team of people who haven't been too closely involved in its development to read through it and to offer constructive ideas for improving your content.

And make sure that the offer that you're making to the customer has been given the necessary management approval before you send the proposal out.

10

THE PROPOSAL PRESENTATION

Presenting your proposal effectively
after submission

Introduction
The eight-stage process for proposal presentations
Summary: the proposal presentation

INTRODUCTION

> *Suppliers will submit their proposals by midday on 15 February. They will then be invited to present their proposal to our evaluation team the following week. Each bidder will be given two hours to present and to answer our questions.*

You've sent in a great proposal, and now they want to see you face-to-face. Ideally, you'll have started thinking about the pitch in parallel with developing the proposal. But the chances are that you'll have been so busy working on the document that you might not get to focus too much on the presentation until the proposal's gone in.

One factor to consider very early on, though: if you do think that there's a chance that you'll have to present, who will be in your presentation team, and when might the presentation take place? As you'll probably want to involve some of your senior managers, the sooner you can get an idea of provisional presentation dates from the customer, the better – so that you can at least start to hold time in the relevant diaries.

"The purpose of the oral presentation is to determine if the buyer can work with the bidder. Selecting key employees is important. Presentation material must be catchy, consistent, professional and cogent. Like the proposal, the presentation material should make the case for why pick 'me'. It is never enough to say 'I'm qualified.' So is everyone else. The point is 'Pick me because I'm different.' In the end, the bidder must give the contracting officer an excuse to pick them over everyone else."
—*Capital & construction director, government department*

"In today's risk-averse world where decisions are increasingly consensus-based, the proposal is even more important in the context of winning business. So for the bidder, ensuring consistency and marrying the sales effort to the proposal to the pitch is vital."
—*David Blume, VP Sales, Qvidian*

In this chapter, we're going to work through eight steps that you need to follow to design, develop and deliver an effective proposal presentation. We're going to focus on the content and process – rather than on the 'stage skills' associated with presenting (much as voice, stance, posture and suchlike are all important).

As we go through the plan, you'll see that – broadly speaking – the process for developing the proposal presentation is simply a microcosm of the overall process that you've just followed to create the proposal itself.

1. *Capture customer requirements & expectations*

They've asked you to present – so it's not unreasonable to ask the customer for some clues as to what they're expecting.

What's their objective for the session? Is this simply a 'we'd like to put faces to the names in your team' session? Do they want to hear a summary of your proposal 'from the horses' mouths'? Are they looking for a detailed working discussion – turning the pages through the proposal and asking specific clarification questions? What mix do they want between formal presentation, discussion and 'Q&A'?

Seek feedback on the proposal that you've submitted. Are there any specific areas on which they'd especially like you to focus during the presentation? Are there any particular topics or sections of the proposal that they're going to want to discuss, or any comments or concerns they'd like you to address?

What about the attendees? Who's going to be there from their side (and what are their roles in their evaluation and approvals process)? How many of your people are they expecting to attend; many customers even impose a maximum limit. Are there any specific staff that they'd like to see in attendance from your side?

And, as always, it's helpful to understand the competitive land-scape. How many other vendors are presenting? Will this be *all* of the suppliers who submitted proposals, or will they already have whittled the field down to a shortlist who came near the top of their initial evaluation? What's the running order on the day – and can you influence this? Many bid teams prefer to go first or last.

Finally at this stage, try and work out what style you think they'll adopt during the session. Will it be friendly, open, hospitable, with them genuinely treating you as a potential 'partner' – or will you find them with their arms folded, hostile, cynical and expecting you to 'get on with it'?

2. *Build your presentation team*

If you're lucky (or, rather, persuasive!), you should have been able to get a clear view from the customer as to the line-up they'd like to see from your organisation. If not, try to work out:

Who would you want to see at the presentation if you were the client?
- Senior management – a Director and / or the Executive Sponsor, at least for large opportunities. The customer will take this as an indication of how seriously you're taking them and this opportunity, how valued they are as a customer and how committed you are to winning and delivering the project. Their presence at this stage may encourage the customer to think that your senior management would be visible, active and accessible if you were selected.
- The salesperson who owns the opportunity – of course! As owner of the relationship and the proposed solution, they need to be there.
- Whoever will be responsible for implementing the solution. (In the customer's mind: 'Can we trust them to deliver? Could we work successfully with this individual?')
- Core team members for major areas (*e.g.* pricing, implementation, technical, support) – taking a steer from the customer if possible as to how technical the presentation should be, and

how detailed the conversation is likely to get.
- Anyone from your business whom they already know well and like, and who may help to establish rapport and credibility on the day.

How many people do they expect to attend – or, if they don't express a preference, how many do you think would be most appropriate? (Strike a careful balance here: you don't want it to feel 'like the army's showed up', but you need to show how committed your company is to being selected and to delivering this successfully.)

Based on the above, work out who's in your line-up. Identify 'reserves' just in case any of the team is unable to attend. And then make sure the team are clear on their respective remits and roles:
- Do make sure that all participants are briefed with key background about the customer, your existing relationship, this opportunity and the likely audience members.
- Do make sure that everyone has read the relevant documents – the customer's RFP, your proposal (from cover to cover) and any relevant internal documentation.
- Do make sure everyone understands the overall strategy and key themes that you embedded in the proposal.
- Check that all members of the team are confident, comfortable presenters. (If not, get them the necessary coaching before they go in front of the customer!)
- Inject some passion into the team. Customers like to listen to suppliers who seem enthusiastic, and who evidently want the business (without seeming *too* desperate for it!).

3. *Design your presentation content*

Remember, unless the customer has indicated otherwise, the primary objective here is to bring your proposal to life, and to clarify any areas where the customer may have questions. At this stage, we'd recommend that you bring at least the core members of the presentation team together to map out the order and content of your presentation. Start by considering what you want your audience to be saying to each other at the conclusion of your presentation.

What do you want them to think regarding your level of commitment, your offer and your capability to implement the solution and achieve the desired results?

Consider the media that you'll use: how are you going to deliver your presentation. Most likely, you'll want to deliver the presentation using PowerPoint, but do consider whether there may be better alternatives.

Now, structure your content. Remember the overall strategy and themes on which you based your proposal? They should have left the customer in no doubt as to 'why you, why not the competition'. The presentation should now complement and correspond to your proposal.

As a guide, you might like to work through the following in order – but remember, this is only a guide: *do* vary it to ensure that it's appropriate for the customer and opportunity in question:

1. Thank them for the opportunity to present and for their time. Briefly introduce the team, highlighting the role and credentials of those present within the project and the presentation.
2. Explain how your presentation is structured, and how long it will take. Encourage them to ask questions as you go through.
3. Provide an overview of their project, their requirements, the expected benefits and what will make for success (slanting this towards your competitive strengths).
4. Give a brief introduction to your capabilities and track record, linking straight into your strategy and key themes.
5. Provide an overview of the offer that you've detailed in your proposal, describing the value it will bring to the customer.
6. Expand on each of your key themes in detail, with evidence.
7. Summarise; re-confirm your enthusiasm and commitment; invite their questions.

For each section, work out what you need to *present* – obviously you can't just cut and paste the proposal text onto a slide and read it out. So, storyboard the presentation: rough out a sketch of what you want to say on each slide and ideas as to how you want the slide laid out on the page. Then work out who's best-placed to present each slide to give it maximum effect – and, if you do have multiple presenters, be clear on how they'll hand over from one to another.

Work out how much time you want to allocate to the various sections, so you're comfortable that you can deliver your messages in the time available. Allow some contingency, and work out what you'd ditch if your time is cut down on the day.

Finally, brainstorm the questions that your audience may throw at you and map out your answers – identifying who will be responsible for responding to each. It's really helpful to ask yourself:
· What are the ten most likely questions they could ask?
· What are the ten most difficult questions they could ask?
· What's the one question we really hope they don't ask? (That's the one they probably will – and you'll want to have a great response to it, rather than floundering in front of them.)

4. *Develop materials*

Next, you'll need to develop the presentation slides themselves.

Remember, you don't want to drown people in information! High-impact slides don't provide a script for the presenter. Instead, they capture the reader's attention, and provide a backdrop for the discussion that needs to take place. As a result, there are two simple design rules that we try to adhere to when designing presentations:
a) A clear, relevant graphic
b) Only as many words as are strictly necessary – and the fewer the better.

If at all possible at this point, commandeer the support of someone who's expert with your presentation software (*e.g.* PowerPoint) and who has a good eye for graphic design and layout. And bear in mind that you may well be able to re-use graphics that you included in the proposal itself.

"A great proposal pitched badly can lose you the deal. Conversely, if you get it just right then you can win. People buy people. So even if your solution has some drawbacks, the way you pitch it and how the customer responds can make or break the deal."
—Sandy Pullinger PPM.APMP, Managing Director, nFold, South Africa

5. *Plan logistics*

For a presentation to go well, you must consider all of the details carefully in advance. A sensible degree of paranoia is essential at this stage – you really can't afford to get this wrong if you want to win the bid.

Walk through the presentation in your mind from start to finish, visualising what will happen from the moment the team meets up on the day, through arrival on the customer's site, right through to the moment you leave. And then think about the risks at each stage, and what you will do to avoid these turning into horribly embarrassing deal-losing catastrophes:

PROPOSAL PRESENTATION PLANNING QUESTIONS

1. Venue
- · Where will the presentation be given?
- · How many people will be attending?
- · How will the room be set out?
- · Will you be able to gain access to the room in advance of the presentation, to set up?

2. Arrival information
- · When should your team arrive?
- · Where are they going to meet?
- · Who's the main point of contact in your team in the event of any problems or issues?
- · Who should you ask for when you arrive? (Remember that your usual contact may well be locked away in the presentation room, and hence not contactable by the customer's receptionist.)

3. Equipment
- · What kit will be required? (Don't just think about what will be needed if all goes well: a key consideration is the need for back-up and a recovery plan in case equipment fails.)

4. Hand-outs
- · What will you leave with the customer? (*e.g.* copies of the presentation, business cards *etc.*)
---

6. Rehearse

The more you prepare and rehearse, the more your presentation will appear to be spontaneous and fresh. It's not enough simply for team members to work out what they're actually going to *say* on the fly when they stand up in front of the customer's team.

We therefore recommend that you run through your presentation in advance – firstly just with the presenters, and then (if at all possible)

THE PROPOSAL PRESENTATION

with a mock audience. For this 'dress rehearsal', ask co-workers to play the role of the customer team. Lay the room out in the way you expect the presentation room to be set up. Walk in, shake hands, set up – just as you will on the day. Present. Let the audience ask questions, and challenge your answers. Try to make the experience as realistic as possible.

And then review – ask the audience to highlight areas where your presentation isn't as clear as it could be and where you might be presenting too little or too much information. Ask them what impressed them, and where you need to sharpen your act.

Ideally, try to ensure that at least some of those present haven't been too involved in the development of your proposal: that way, they'll be able to provide a degree of objectivity that the team may have started to lose after working on the material together for so long. It can be especially useful if you can persuade someone who has experience on the purchasing side of the negotiating table to sit in and pretend to be one of the customer's team – they'll usually bring a fresh perspective and a degree of healthy cynicism that may be of value!

7. *Deliver*

So you've come to the day of the presentation:
- Make sure everyone is clear where to meet and when, and that you have contingency plans 'just in case'.
- If at all possible, do a brief run-through immediately prior to the presentation. At the very least, last-minute reminders should be given:
  - Make good eye contact.
  - Speak clearly and confidently.
  - 'Why us, why not them.'
  - Remember: you are a guest.
- Assign someone in the team – not the person leading the presentation – to set up the equipment as required.
- Lights, music, action! Give the presentation your best shot – after all, you'll have rehearsed it professionally, so it should by

now come naturally and be a great success. Take your time and don't rush. If you've properly prepared, you'll have plenty of time to deliver your presentation.

- Watch the customer side for their reactions to the presentation. Ideally, have individual team members assigned to watch a specific audience member and to monitor and note their reactions. Their body language can give away powerful clues, and these can be discussed discreetly (*e.g.* during breaks); adjustments can then be made if needed to the presentation and delivery to ensure it is received as well as possible.
- You should have determined in advance how questions during the presentation will be handled. One sound method is to have one person take all the questions, and then direct the appropriate person to answer it. When taking questions, remember not to rush to answer them. And if you don't know the answer, don't attempt to 'bluff' or 'tap dance' your way through one. It is perfectly acceptable and preferable to say, 'That's a very astute question and I think we'll need some time to look into that and get an answer for you.'
- Don't forget to thank the customer's team at the end of the presentation for their time, interest and hospitality.

8. *Review*

As soon as possible after the presentation, meet and review the session. Discuss the reactions of the customer's evaluation team, using any notes that were taken, and the questions / concerns that may have been raised. Assign follow-up activities (*e.g.* to complete any actions agreed with the customer during the presentation) as appropriate. And seek feedback as soon as possible from the customer (if it's appropriate to do so).

Your proposal should have established you at the front of the pack trying to win the deal and have secured you an invitation to present; presenting it well should confirm you as the customer's bidder of choice.

Yet too often, bid teams turn up to the presentation under-prepared and under-rehearsed. A carefully-planned approach, with well-crafted presentation materials, really pays dividends! Just as with developing the proposal itself, there's a structured process to follow that can ensure success.

"It's not just about the written proposal. It's about how you say what you need to say at the presentation, and making sure you have a heavyweight team there on the day who are well coordinated and prepared, and articulate fully and properly what's been said in the proposal."
—*Procurement director, financial services*

"The primary purpose of the pitch to the customer is for them to see if they trust you. People buy from people they trust and like."
—*Jay Herther (APMP Fellow / Professional & Author, USA)*

LEARNING REVIEW

Helping to win future deals

In this chapter §

INTRODUCTION

Every bid can generate significant learning opportunities for your organisation: how well did you fare versus the competition; what helped or hindered the team?

Capturing this learning, identifying actions and recommendations, and feeding these back to appropriate senior management to get support and drive improvements, are essential for successful bidding organisations. After all, if you have found things that work, then *others* may find them useful too; if you've had problems in any area, then you're going to want them addressed before *you* next work on a bid!

This section discusses 'Learning Reviews'. Not 'inquests' or 'post-mortems'. Not 'loss reviews'. The intent is *not* to find a scapegoat, lay blame or point fingers.

There are opportunities to learn, win or lose. If you've won, you're going to want to celebrate your success – and capture anything you did that your organisation might want to replicate on future opportunities and embed more widely. Even though you've captured the deal, there'll probably still be things that were a little too close for comfort, that you'd do differently next time.

If you've lost the deal – we're sorry to hear that. You need to review what took place and identify improvements that might help future losses. And at the same time, you need to reflect on any good things that went on: there are bound to have been some!

We'd suggest that you run a Learning Review shortly after submitting and presenting your proposal – whilst everything is fresh in the team members' minds. And then, once you've heard the results of the client's deliberations, seek out their feedback and reconvene the team to see what additional learning results from their comments.

Remember: hindsight is a wonderful thing. It's likely that everyone working on your proposal did the best job on it that they felt they could at the time, given the other work and life pressures that they may have been facing. Respect this, and keep the discussion positive!

"A debrief after a win can be more valuable than after a loss."
—*Jane Matthews, Head of Bids & Tender, Aviva Life*

If you can get feedback from the customer before your internal learning review, so much the better. But as we've just mentioned, you may want to get on and review learning before you've had a client debrief. After all, it can sometimes take weeks or months for them to make their decision, following a long period of negotiation and due diligence. And if you wait until they're ready to talk, people will have forgotten what went on during the proposal effort – and you'll have missed opportunities to put any learning into practice in the interim.

Recognising that you may not have that much time for the discussion when it does take place, here's a list of some of the key things to cover:

FEEDBACK TOPICS	CLIENT COMMENTS

1. Your offer: strengths & weaknesses of your offer against other bidders:
    a. Solution
    b. Implementation / timescales
    c. Legal / commercials
    d. Financials / likely benefits
    e. Other issues.	

2. Bid engagement:
    a. Quality and responsiveness of engagement throughout the bid
    b. Professionalism of any meetings, visits *etc.*
    c. Handling of negotiation phase.	

FEEDBACK TOPICS	CLIENT COMMENTS

3. Your proposal:
   a. Quality and impact of proposal (*e.g.* easy to evaluate? client focused? well-written and presented? clear, compelling, differentiated story?)
   b. What were the client's evaluation criteria and how did you perform against these?
   c. Strengths and weaknesses compared to other bidders
   d. What could you have done to make a better impact or scored higher?
   e. Professionalism in handling follow-up / clarification questions.	

4. Your proposal presentation:
   a. Quality and impact of presentation
   b. Feedback on the presentation team (individually / collectively)
   c. Strengths and weaknesses compared to the other bidders
   d. What could you have done to make a better impact or score higher?	

"We see all sorts of quality from suppliers. The average is not great. The ones that stand out are those that are tailored and look unique to the situation."
—*Director of procurement, services sector*

A few useful questions to have up your sleeve might include:
- How did you rate our chances of success from the outset of the bid?
- Did you get to meet the right people during the process?
- Was any team member outstanding – or disappointing?
- What was the one thing that, more than anything else, won (or lost) us the deal?
- If we were to do one thing differently next time we bid to you, what should that be?

Given the sensitivity of some of the discussions, we recommend that someone other than the account manager meets the customer for this debrief session. After all, the client may have built too close a relationship with that individual to feel comfortable offering fully frank feedback – and the salesperson may have a vested interest in skewing any feedback received to demonstrate that, depending on the outcome, 'it was all down to me' or 'it wasn't my fault'!

RUNNING THE REVIEW

Characteristics of a great learning review include that it:
- Involves all those who played a significant part in pursuing the opportunity.
- Provides all participants with the opportunity to contribute honestly and openly, without feeling fear of reprisal or the need to defend themselves.
- Has an *independent* facilitator – someone who has the necessary skills, who wasn't involved in the bid, and who has nothing personal to gain / lose from the likely recommendations.
- Takes the necessary amount of time to complete, and isn't rushed. (Hey, if you've spent weeks working on a bid, a few hours more to help to make it easier next time around isn't *too* much to ask, is it?!)
- Honours what went well, highlighting appropriate positive feedback.
- Treats anything that didn't go well as an opportunity to improve, not a reason for blame.
- Sticks to the facts, rather than feelings – for example 'two

major deliverables were three days late' rather than 'I felt like you didn't care about sticking to the agreed plan'.

· Where any issues are raised regarding the performance of individuals within the team, ensures that these are kept confidential within the team and not shared publicly unless agreed by all concerned – whilst looking for ways to ensure that similar issues could be avoided in future.
· Captures customer and competitive information that may be useful for future bids.
· Communicates appropriate learning and recommendations clearly to relevant stakeholders in the business.
· Leads to a clear list of actions and recommendations, each with identified sponsor(s) and owner(s), with clear timescales – thus ensuring that real action *does* take place as a result.
· Drives improvements that do lead to real enhancements in capability and future effectiveness and efficiency.

So, get the team together: the people who worked on this opportunity. Clearly, you'll have to use common sense here – if someone's only spent ten minutes helping you with one answer in your proposal, you may not need to take up their time – unless that one answer won or lost you the deal, or they should have been more actively involved! And, in practice, you may need to solicit some participants' comments by email prior to the review session.

Explain the objectives of the meeting to them, and establish some shared ground-rules – for example, the behaviours that the team will adopt during the review, and they may need some coaching on the language that's appropriate for a constructive session:

GOOD PHRASES TO USE	PHRASES TO AVOID
SUCCESSES	*BLAME*
ACHIEVED	*I FEEL*
RECOMMENDATION	*FAULT*
IMPROVEMENT OPPORTUNITY	*FAILURES*
HONEST	*YOU SHOULD HAVE …*
CONSTRUCTIVE	*YOU DIDN'T …*

"During each proposal it is good to keep a log of interesting events that generate 'lessons learnt'. I always issue a 'What went right, what went wrong' document (2–3 pages) at the end of a proposal, gathering feedback from the core bid team. When starting a new proposal, I take a few minutes to read such a document and then I keep it handy."
—*Claudiu Blejdea, Bid Manager, Alcatel-Lucent, Romania*

The agenda might usefully include the following:

AGENDA ITEM
1. Introductions, objectives, ground rules.
2. What happened? (Brief recap of the bid / proposal timeline and activities.)
3. What was the outcome?
4. What feedback have we had from the customer?
5. What worked well and what could be improved in each of the following areas: · our **sales / business development** approach · our **proposal management** approach and the quality of documents we submit · our **solution** – product offerings, services, infrastructure, systems, operations, implementation, support *etc.* · our **commercial and financial** offering – pricing, benefits, contractual.
6. What recommendations do we wish to make – to whom and when?

Recognising that some issues may be sensitive for some participants (and that some participants may tend to dominate the discussion at the expense of quieter members of the team), you may also want to use other techniques to draw out each contributor's views, such as:

· Asking team members to write their comments on post-it notes, then displaying, grouping and discussing these.
· Displaying topics on flipcharts around the room, and allowing team members to walk between them and record comments anonymously, before discussing them as a group.
· Interviewing 'sensitive' team members before the Learning Review, drawing out the major issues; the facilitator can then

introduce these more 'controversial' topics as discussion points, without putting any individual team member on the spot.

- Using prompts to draw out information, such as:
  - What was your personal high point / low point working on this bid?
  - What was the main reason we won / lost?
  - What's the biggest barrier that needs to be overcome in future bids?

And if it's a smaller proposal effort, with just a few of you involved – or if you simply can't get the whole team together due to (for example) geography, then it's still important to run a review. Consider doing the review as a conference call. Or, at least, send an email to all who were involved asking them to list two or three things they think went especially well, and two or three that might need to be done differently in future.

"Professional proposal writers are one of the scarcest commodities in our industry. If you have a good one in your team, nurture them, embrace them, learn from them and give them the space they need to be creative. They really can make the difference between winning and losing."
—*Martin Smith, Managing Director, Bid Solutions*

Once you've captured and prioritised the team's input – remembering that your recommendations can, of course, be things that other teams should replicate, as well as things that need to be changed – you'll need to circulate it to all involved, and to present it. *Senior management, here we come!*

If the deal was significant enough, or the recommendations might require significant changes within the business, you need (and deserve) a senior-level audience for your output – with people who can drive change. Your bosses *should* welcome (and expect) your input. So go and talk to them – either one-on-one with key individuals, or by presenting at one of their meetings – and ask them what they're going to do to sponsor and help implement any recommendations.

Whilst it's not really in the scope of this document to discuss how your company structures its overall proposal capabilities, there are some common tactics that successful sales teams follow to optimise their bidding efficiency and effectiveness. Rather than abandoning the salesperson who receives the RFP to pull together a response himself or herself, many companies have a professional Proposal Centre to provide support and steer the team through the process.

If you don't yet have such a team, you might want to consider establishing a more systemic approach which ticks the following boxes:

· skilled, experienced, well-trained proposal staff – where possible, accredited by APMP (the Association of Proposal Management Professionals) – to assist with larger and more strategic opportunities
· a clear, realistic engagement model and capacity plan for the proposal centre, showing which (and how many) deals they can support and the service they'll provide
· training in the necessary proposal skills for all those involved in proposal development
· a comprehensive library of pre-written, proposal-ready content

that is accurate, up-to-date, well-written and approved – and which addresses a significant proportion of the frequently asked questions in the RFPs you receive

- professional-looking design templates, that are easy to use and easy to tailor to the needs of the specific customer and opportunity
- a clear governance process, covering (at least) qualification and approvals
- a strong infrastructure to enable sales staff to develop their own proposals where the central team doesn't have the resource to help – including training and access to templates, content and production facilities.

SUMMARY: LEARNING REVIEW

A well-run learning review will help you to:
- capture vital customer and competitor information
- improve the products and services that you offer
- improve your proposal capabilities and the overall bidding process
- honour the good work that took place
- win future bids.

So, win or lose, do capture the views of the key participants in the bid, and feed these through to the senior management who need to sponsor or deliver any improvement recommendations.

"I've learnt more through effective win / loss reviews with customers than by any other means. Decisions are never black and white and you will always get more information verbally than written down because people become more honest and forthcoming when they talk to you and if you ask the right questions. We've been told how our pricing or solution stacks up at a very granular level and the feedback is essential for us to better position our next bid. Don't be scared to ask – all they can do is say no and you have lost nothing – and more often than not you get a lot more information than you expected."
—*Kathryn Wyon,*
Head of Sales Advisory,
Lloyds Bank, UK

IN CONCLUSION
Apply this and win!

We hope you've found this book useful in understanding how to adopt a more strategic approach to producing winning proposals. We certainly hope that it will give you some fresh ideas and inspiration with regard to proposal creation.

We've recommended that you're a tad ruthless in selecting which deals to chase, via a robust qualification process. We've explored the value of pre-proposal planning, in helping to maximise your chance of success before the customer even asks you to produce a proposal. We've talked about proposal strategy (the three Cs, leading to a clear understanding of 'why us, why not them').

We've suggested that you 'storyboard' answers to each question before you start writing (for example, using the 'questions to answer questions' and 'three-star answers' techniques), to ensure that you maximise your scores in the client's evaluation. And we've given you some hints and tips on proposal writing styles. We've talked about document management, presentations and learning reviews.

Put another way, we want you to be the leading contender at every stage of the customer's journey evaluating your and your competitors' proposals. Over the page is a charter for you to refer to when working on your next deal.

The customer will expect my organisation *to win,* before they receive the bidders' proposals.

When the proposal documents from different vendors sit on the meeting room table in front of the evaluators, ours will **STAND OUT FROM** *the crowd before they've even read a word of the text.*

The cover of our proposal will *persuade* them that ours is the document that will capture their hearts and minds.

As they scan through the documents for the first time – flicking through the pages, their eyes alighting only on the titles and *graphics* — they'll be convinced that ours is going to be the best.

By the time they've finished the Table of Contents, they'll be excited about reading the rest of the document: section titles alone will demonstrate our **understanding** *and our* **differentiation.**

The Executive Summary will get the evaluators on our side quickly, propelling us *clearly ahead of our* competitors.

Our responses to each question or requirement will re-confirm our compelling story, *expanding on and validating our win themes.*

Our conclusions section will ensure that they close the book with our

key themes

clearly in mind, certain

that they want to choose us.

Our proposal presentation will reinforce their decision that

we're the people with whom

— *they want to do business.* —

Most importantly of all, we've encouraged you to think more strategically about your entire approach to proposal development. It's about much more than just typing your answers, and submitting a complete and compliant document, on time. It's about submitting proposals that present a clear and compelling value proposition that differentiates you from your competitors. It's about ensuring that your story is superbly articulated. It's about hitting the right notes for the customer's evaluation and decision-making teams. And, as a result, it's about winning more business – and winning more easily!

As we said at the outset: good luck – and now you have some tactics you can use to shape that luck in your favour ...

INDEX

Jon Williams and BJ Lownie are the Principal Directors of Strategic Proposals. Their practical, efficient and highly effective approach to developing proposals is used by clients across many industries worldwide. Their award-winning work has taken them to over thirty countries, with a win rate of over 80%.

Both Jon and BJ are *Fellows of the Association of Proposal Management Professionals* (APMP). Together, they write *The Proposal Guys*, the acclaimed proposal management blog. They have presented at numerous conferences and publish articles on proposals on a regular basis; they are widely recognised for their passion for the subject and their thought leadership in the proposal profession.

Before setting up Strategic Proposals' European operation in 2001, Jon set up and ran Compaq's Strategic Bid Centre. Previously, he held a number of senior procurement roles, and he served as a board director of international purchasing consultancy PMMS.

BJ started his career in journalism in New York City, before moving into the business world and heading the proposal centre for Digital Equipment Corporation. He founded P3, the precursor to Strategic Proposals, in 1988, and has since worked with clients on every continent except Antarctica. (He's still waiting for that gig!)

When not working on proposals Jon is most likely to be found in a bookstore or at the opening of a new hotel. BJ will be found at a dog park or on a mountain.

Strategic Proposals' 25-strong team operates from offices in the US, UK and Netherlands – and works with partners around the world in countries including Australia, Germany and South Africa. Services include benchmarking, improving clients' proposal capabilities, training, professional accreditation for bid / proposal staff, and live deal support.